John and Pat Underwood

walk & eat

A

CONTENTS

This pocket guide is designed for short-break walking holidays on Madeira, using public transport (or a car, if you prefer). Funchal, the capital, is easily and fairly inexpensively reached by charter flights, and the climate makes for brilliant walking all year round.

Fly out for just a week. You have in your hand enough walks, excursions, restaurants and recipes to last two weeks — so you can pick and choose the most appealing.

The highlights at a glance:

- 13 varied day walks, each with topographical map
- 2 excursions — one just a short 'flight' by cable car, the other a fairly long bus ride, with walks from each
- recommended restaurants and hotels
- recipes to make at your self-catering base or back home
- special section with hints on wheat-, gluten- and dairy-free eating and cooking on the island

INTRO

THE WALKS

The walks in this book (a 'baker's dozen') range from easy, flat routes along *levadas* (irrigation channels) to moderate hillside hikes. Dotted round the island (see map on pages 126-127), they have been chosen because they are *easily reached by bus and there is good eating en route.* For a very wide selection of island walks, we recommend *Landscapes of Madeira,* with over 100 different routes. Now in its eleventh edition, the book has been the 'walkers' Bible' for 30 years and was the first of Sunflower's 'Landscapes' guides. This series now covers 50 destinations. For more information see www.sunflowerbooks.co.uk.

THE EXCURSIONS

Two 'days out' are described. The first is just a short cable car ride to the hills above Funchal, where you can visit some lovely gardens and have lunch. It's an outing in itself, but also the jumping-off point for Walks 1 and 2. The second excursion, much beloved of users of *Landscapes of Madeira,* is a bus trip that takes in the north and west of the island. A four-hour stop for lunch at Porto Moniz allows you plenty of time to swim in the attractive lido — preferably *after* doing Walk 13.

THE RESTAURANTS

We have *featured* the restaurants (and hotels) we use regularly and say why we like them. In each case we include a 'mini-menu' listing some of their specialities. A price guide is given (€ to €€€) to indicate 'very reasonable' to 'fairly pricey'. But remember that you can have a relatively inexpensive meal in a five-star hotel if you just have a light lunch. At the Quinta do Furão, for example, we paid just 24 € for two soups, a tray of grilled limpets shared between two and a full bottle of wine. They also offer a tray of free 'nibbles' while you wait.

Hints: A modest **tip** is included in your bill, but plan on adding another 5-10% to reward good service. Many of our restaurants have **free wifi**. *No restaurant has paid in cash or kind to be included in this guide.*

> If you would like to know more about Madeiran recipes, look out for a book called *Secrets of Madeira Cooking* by Zita Cardoso (available in most souvenir shops). Delia Smith has no competition here; the 'secrets' remain secret (some ingredients are missing and there are no oven temperatures or cooking times), *but* the book is fascinating nevertheless, with a huge variety of recipes — an unending source of inspiration! While it was written in cooperation with the Madeira Hotel School, unfortunately you will search the island's restaurants in vain for most of these dishes.

Some of the restaurants are at hotels where you might like to spend the night, especially if you want to have dinner there and there is no public transport back to base later in the evening.

THE RECIPES

Most of our recommended restaurants were willing to share with us the *ingredients* used in their recipes, but the actual preparation remains their 'secret' (in truth, they are simply not written down, but just passed on from cook to cook over the years). So you can rest assured that we have cooked *all* of the given recipes ourselves, to make sure they 'work'!

What we cannot guarantee, of course, is that they will taste as good back home as they did on Madeira! So many factors come into play to make food taste better when you are on holiday — from the intangibles (the atmosphere and the sense of relaxation after a day's good walking) to the tangible (hardness of the water, quality of the fish and other ingredients — even bananas!). So if you are in self-catering, why not try some of these recipes while you're on the island?

We've made all of these dishes on the simple kind of cooker usually found in self-catering (two rings and a decent oven) — or on a barbecue. And good news for anyone suffering food intolerances: all of the recipes can be **gluten- and dairy-free** (see page 136).

MADEIRAN FOOD

You will be hard-pressed to have a bad meal on the island if you seek out 'regional' (Madeiran) dishes. Top of our list would be **soup**: the ubiquitous tomato and onion, fresh vegetable (varied daily), or thick fish soups. **Fish** dishes are always reliable, from plain grills to *espada* with exotic

On virtually every café menu you will find *prego* (steak sandwich). The *prego* shown above left is on *bolo do caco* (see page 82) — *not* a good idea, since the thick bread overwhelms the thin piece of steak; *prego* is far better on a simple roll *(papa seco)*. If you don't fancy a sandwich, there's always *prego no prato* (steak and fried egg on a plate, shown above right) — with chips and salad.

fruit. **Beef** (including the speciality, *espetada*) ranges from perfection to shoe leather. There is no better beef than Madeiran, but *do* make sure your beef is sirloin *(lombo)* or fillet *(filete)*.

Pork and **chicken** also feature widely and are invariably best when grilled on open fires (as, for instance, at the Eira do Serrado or Curral das Freiras; see Walk 3). Do *not* expect to find many veal or lamb dishes, although some of our recommended restaurants do offer lamb cutlets.

We tend to give the **dessert** course a miss; in simple restaurants these are usually limited to *pudim* (a sort of crème caramel) or fruit. But some of our recommendations *do* have exotic sweets or cakes, mentioned on the mini-menus.

'**Madeira-style**' on a menu invariably means with tomato and onion ... probably a bit of garlic, and perhaps oregano.

Table wines are imported from Portugal, with the exception of a few fairly new wines from vineyards in Porto Moniz and São Vicente, which

Portuguese wines

All supermarkets stock good wines from mainland Portugal. Some of our favourites are those from the mountains north of Oporto (including fortified ports):
• *Vinho Verde* ('green', or new wine): slightly sparkling quaffing wine — Aveleda, Casal Garcia, Gatão and Lagosta
• *Douro* — Esteva, Evel, Ferreirinho, Planalto, Porça de Murça
• *Bairrada* — Aliança, João Pires, José-Maria Fonseca BSE (Branco Seco Especial)
From further south, around Coimbra, there are reliable heavy reds
• *Dão* — Grão Vasco, Terras Altas
Other perennial favourites come from areas closer to Lisbon:
• *Alentejo* — Monsaraz, Monte Velho, Porta da Ravessa
• *Ribatejo* — Serradayres
• *Setúbal* — Perequita
• *Beira* — Quinta do Cardo white

Glossary

consumo: ordinary wine; *reserva:* better quality; *garrafeira:* best quality; *tinto:* red; *branco:* white; *garrafa:* bottle; *batoque:* cork (in case you want to take it home!)

we have found both expensive and disappointing. See page 113 for a brief introduction to the fortified **madeira wines**.

And finally: most restaurant portions (especially in the inexpensive establishments) are *huge*. They won't mind you sharing a main course. And don't be surprised, in a country restaurant, to be served boiled potatoes, sweet potatoes, rice and bread all with the same dish! Carbohydrate-watchers beware!

PLANNING YOUR VISIT
When to go

The simple answer is — any time of year. The island does not experience such great fluctuations in temperature as the mainland. Winter days are often warm and sunny (up to 20°C), and even at the height of summer the air temperature does not usually rise above 25°C on the coast. But we would suggest avoiding June and early July, when the island is often covered by a low cloud 'hat' — the *capacete*.

An ideal time to travel is at low season (August till Christmas, January 2nd to Easter, and again after Easter until the end of May). Christmas and Easter are high-season — crowded and expensive. *Do* of course, reckon with some days of rain, especially in early spring and autumn.

Where to stay

There is a wide choice of accommodation of all grades all over the island. But for a short, week's break by public transport, it is best to stay around Funchal, from where the buses will take you to all the walks in this book.

Rather than an hotel, consider self-catering: just search 'apartments in Funchal' on the web; Google, for instance, throws up dozens of sites, including privately-owned second homes and hotels with self-catering facilities. There are also several sites dedicated to the island, like madeira-island.com, which have lists of apartments and villas to rent.

What to take

Pack simply! You don't have to 'dress', even for dinner, in any of the restaurants we recommend. Instead, concentrate on your walking gear.

While no special equipment is needed for any of the walks, proper **walking boots** are preferable to any other footwear. Many walks can be wet or slippery at some stage; good ankle support is essential, and you will also be glad of the water-proofing. Each person should carry a **small rucksack**, and *all year round* it is advisable to pack it with a **sunhat, first-aid kit, spare socks** and some **warm clothing**. A **long-sleeved shirt** and **long trousers** should be worn or carried, for sun protection and for making your way through encroaching vegetation (which may be wet and prickly). You should always carry a **mobile phone**; the **emergency** number on Madeira (as throughout the EU) is 112. Note: some walks require a **torch**!

Depending on the season, you may also need a **windproof, lightweight rainwear, fleece** and **gloves**. Optional items include **swimwear** and a Swiss Army knife (packed in your hold luggage, *not* hand-luggage, or it will be confiscated!). Mineral water is sold almost everywhere in plastic half-litre bottles; *it is imperative that each walker carries at least a half-litre of water — a full litre in hot weather.*

Planning your walks

Look over the walks in advance — if only to see if you will need a torch! The walks are specifically designed for access by the excellent local **bus** network ... so that you can enjoy a bottle of wine with lunch! But if you *do* want to hire a **car**, and the route is linear, you can usually leave your car at the end of the walk and take a bus to the start.

Broad beans drying beside a levada. They are eaten dry as a snack or rehydrated to make soups and stews.

We have **graded our walks** for the deskbound person who nevertheless keeps reasonably fit. None of these walks ascends more than about 300m/1000ft, although there are a few steep descents. Remember that these are *neat walking times;* it would be wise to *double the time,* to allow for nature-watching and stopping for a meal.

Our walking **maps** are based on old 1:25,000 and 1:50,000 maps of the island published by the Portuguese government. We have updated these through our own research on foot or by car (for this edition using GPS) and printed them at a scale of 1:35,000. But the only paths shown on our maps are those we *know* to be viable at time of writing.

Walking safely depends in great part on *knowing what to expect and being properly equipped.* For this reason we urge you to read through the *whole* walk description at your leisure *before* setting out, so that you have a mental picture of each stage of the route and the landmarks. A few of the routes are **signposted** or **waymarked** with red and yellow flashes (two horizontal stripes mean *continue this way*; X means *do not go this way*). On *most* of these walks you will encounter other people — an advantage if you get into difficulty. Nevertheless, we advise you **never** to walk alone.

ON ARRIVAL
Tourist information
There is a small tourist information office at the airport (often unstaffed), where you can pick up leaflets. The main tourist office is on Avenida Arriaga (1 on the plan) and open Mon-Fri 09.00-20.00, Sat-Sun 09.00-18.00; (291 225 658. Do stop by to pick up some free island maps and a list of events — unfortunately they no longer supply bus timetables, since this information is now available on the web.

There are many pretty outdoor cafés in Funchal, where you can take a break from shopping.

City bus pass
Horarios do Funchal are the operators of the orange **town buses**, and you'll be amazed how far they will take you! The best bargain is a **7-day pass** (17.50 €) offering unlimited jour-

neys throughout all zones. Otherwise, pay the driver as you board (1.80 € per trip for the inner zone) or use the self-service 'Giro' kiosks to create and top up personal travel cards, saving about 40% on cash prices. Passes are available at several kiosks along the Avenida do Mar (see plan; manned from 08.30 to 18.00 daily). You can download any of the Horarios **timetables** *in advance:* www.horariosdofunchal.pt. There is also an excellent map of all their bus routes on the site.

Madeiran bananas fail EU beauty contests but are sweet and delectable.

Shopping for self-catering

Although more exotic shopping trips will come later, make your first port of call the nearest **supermarket**, to stock up on essentials. Our favourite supermarkets in central Funchal are shown on the plan (at 10 and 21), but there are others just outside the centre and in the larger villages. Aside from staples, you may want to pick up a few extra things that might be missing from your base — like a vegetable peeler, a whisk … or batteries.

All the supermarkets have separate sections for delicatessen items, butchers and fishmongers, as well as bakeries. So this is an easy option if you're shopping in the afternoon or on a Sunday, when local markets aren't usually open. (Most island supermarkets are now open all day, even on Sundays.)

'Regional' produce

The supermarket shopping list (right) is just for staples, but in case you are buying fresh produce as well, here are a few tips.

There are three main supermarket chains: Pingo Doce, Modelo and Sã. In our experience, all are brilliant for buying anything from a packet of crisps to a TV or toaster. But we have listed them in order of *quality of fresh produce*: Pingo Doce is definitely the best in this respect and Sã is often downright poor.

Be careful in supermarkets (and even countryside *mini-mercados*) to buy *fresh Madeiran produce,* as a lot of EU produce is also on sale and, at first glance, may look more attractive. Potatoes are an example. Madeiran potatoes are often sold un-washed, and may seem a little grubby. The skin looks thick, and they sometimes feel soft when you peel them. *But they are fantastic,* and cook beautifully — boiled, roasted, puréed, chipped or baked.

Madeiran produce is usually identified as 'regional'. If in doubt, point to the item

---

Supermarket shopping list reminder

washing-up liquid or dishwasher tablets
paper towels
aluminium foil
soap
tissues/toilet paper
scouring pads
salt & pepper
mineral water
milk/cream*
coffee/tea/drinking chocolate
butter*
sugar
bread*
juice
wine/beer/cider
(olive) oil & vinegar
eggs
tomato purée
rice
mayonnaise/mustard
torch batteries?
vegetable peeler?
whisk?

*see gluten- and dairy-free alternatives on page 138

and ask if it is 'ray-jee-oh-**nahl**'. If it isn't, you may pay considerably more, and you will certainly eat less well.

Mercado dos Lavradores, from top to bottom, left to right: tuna and slinky black *espada* (both a must; they will fillet the *espada* for you); colourful moray eel and dried cod *(bacalhau)* — dare you try either of these? Vegetables and (below) a fanciful display of exotic fruits

Mercado dos Lavradores

Once the staples are in the cupboard, the real shopping fun can begin. It is worth getting up early to visit Funchal's **market** (29 on the plan). It opens Mon-Sat at 07.00 and is a feast for the eyes. Spend a while looking round first, to see what's on offer, then go back to the stalls where you want to buy. The market closes at 16.00 Mon-Thur and 15.00 on Saturdays. If you want to shop quite late, go on a Friday, when it's open till 20.00.

15

This breathtaking 15-20 minute 'flight' is the perfect start to a day sightseeing around Monte. You can return to Funchal by the famous 2km-long 'toboggan run' or by bus, or take another cable car to the Jardim Botânico. Best of all, use the upper station as the starting point for Walk 1 or 2.

monte cable car

EXCURSION

The ride begins at the **lower cable car station** at the eastern end of the Avenida do Mar (37 on the plan). Tickets are fairly pricey, but the panoramic views are worth every euro. Perhaps the most dramatic part of the 'flight' comes as the car rises over the motorway, with views straight down into the green corridor of the João Gomes Valley (Walk 1).

The ride ends at the **upper cable car station** (with café) at **Babosas**, just east of Monte. As you alight, you may be handed a leaflet advertising a 'light lunch' at the five-star **Quinta do Monte** (see page 19). If you are not planning to come back here for lunch or tea, turn *right* outside the

Transport: 🚠 cable car from Funchal to Babosas (near Monte); daily 09.30-18.00 except in strong winds/storms); 15-20min each way (291 780 280; www.madeiracablecar.com
Return the same way (buy a return ticket, it's less expensive) or by frequent town 🚌 20 or 21 from Monte or town 🚌 22 from Babosas — or by toboggan (see below)

Refreshments en route:
Quinta do Monte (see page 19)
Monte Palace Gardens (café)
Cafés at the cable car station and in Monte

Points of Interest:
Monte Church (Nossa Senhora do Monte)
Monte Palace Tropical Garden; Mon-Sat 09.00-18.00; closed holidays (291 782 339
Babosas balcony viewpoint
'Toboggan ride' *(Carros de cesto)*; daily 09.00-18.00 (13.00 Sundays). Not 1/1, Good Friday, 15-16/8, 25/12

cable car station, to enjoy the view Babosas Balcony. Otherwise, turn *left* outside the cable car station. Following the agapanthus-lined Caminho das Babosas, you'll pass the hotel entrance on the right. Even if you don't take up their lunch offer, *do* visit the gardens — entrance is free.

Public gardens at Monte (left), setting off on the toboggan run (right); below: decorating Monte Church for the Feast of the Assumption (15/16 August)

Just opposite, on the left, is the entrance to the **Monte Palace Tropical Garden**, created during the late 1980s by a Madeiran who made his fortune in South Africa. Again, the entry price is fairly steep, but you can spend hours here admiring the wealth of tropical and indigenous plants, not to mention the wonderful ceramic tiles and a host of minor follies.

Further along the lane is the starting point for the **toboggan run**, just below **Monte Church**, where Madeiran pilgrims pray to the tiny poignant statue of Our Lady of the Assumption, the island's patron saint. Beyond the church are the **public gardens**, a delight of topiary laid out below the ivy-covered viaduct of the old funicular railway that once ran between Monte and Funchal. In the **main square** plane trees shade a bandstand, cafés, souvenir stalls and taxis galore.

Head back east from the square, to return by toboggan, cable car or bus from Babosas — or to carry on with Walk 1 or 2. We highly recommend stopping for a snack, lunch or tea at the Quinta do Monte. Even if you're wearing walking boots, you will be welcome in the gardens or the tile-floored Winter Garden (pictured).

Babosas is just a plane-shaded square with a bus shelter and a superb viewpoint over **Curral dos Romeiros** (see photograph on page 20). There used to be a lovely 19th-century chapel here, but it was swept away in the devastating mudslides of February 2010.

Winter Garden at the Quinta do Monte

QUINTA DO MONTE
Largo das Babosas (291 780 100
www.quintamonte.com
daily, all day €–€€

3-course **'light lunch'** — soup or salad, steak with potatoes and fresh vegetables, tropical fruit salad €€

superb **snack menu** from 2,50 € — including a dozen different sand-wiches, toasted sandwiches, salads, cakes, hot snacks like crêpes, ome-lettes, quiche and spaghetti

drinks from 2,50 €. The hot cho-colate is a perfect warmer before setting off on Walks 1 or 2.

One of the things that has always amazed us about Madeira is how close you can be to dense housing yet come upon a primeval landscape just around a fold in the hillside. This walk is a perfect example; it explores the 'Green Corridor' created by the awesome João Gomes Valley.

ribeira de joão gomes

WALK

Babosas and Monte from the João Gomes valley

The walk starts from the **upper cable car station** at **Babosas**. When you leave the glassed-in station, turn right. (But if you first want to visit Monte or have a warming drink at the Quinta do Monte, turn left; see page 19.) Almost at once you come to a balcony viewpoint overlooking the wild, deep João Gomes Valley — where you are heading.

Go down the walkway to the Jardim Botânico cable car (various signs, including 'Levada dos Tornos', 'Bom Sucesso'), then follow the trail below the station. Some 350m/yds below Babosas, you come to a fork (**7min**). The main walk keeps straight on (left) here on an earthen path signed 'Levada dos Tornos'. *(Those who don't have a*

Distance: 6km/3.7mi; 2h35min

Grade: moderate-strenuous, with a very steep descent of 400m/1300ft (mostly on steps). *Hard on the knees. Not suitable after rain.* Short initial ascent to the Levada dos Tornos (90m/300ft). You must be sure-footed and have a head for heights; possibility of vertigo on the levadas (but the first vertiginous section can be omitted; see notes at the 7min-point).

Equipment: stout lace-up shoes or walking boots, warm clothing in cool weather, walking stick(s)

Transport: 🚡 cable car (see page 17) or town 🚌 22 to Babosas. Return on town 🚌 7, 29, 30, 33, 34A, 36 or 47 from Bom Sucesso

Refreshments en route:
Quinta do Monte (see page 19) or café at one of the cable car stations (all three at the start of the walk) bar at Bom Sucesso at the end

Points of Interest:
Babosas balcony viewpoint
Levada dos Tornos
'Green Corridor' flora

head for heights might like to follow the main walk 90m/300ft up to the levada, to see the setting and the waterfall. Then return to this fork to continue. Otherwise, curl sharp right downhill now, keeping to the main trail with street lights (sign: 'Curral dos Romeiros, Levada do

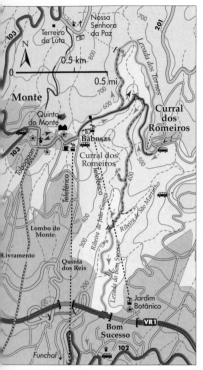

Bom Sucesso'). Follow this across a bridge over the João Gomes River, rise up the far side and then fork right at the sign 'Levada do Bom Sucesso', to rejoin the main walk at the 1h05min-point.)

The main walk path climbs gently for 90m/300ft to join the **Levada dos Tornos** (see page 30) at the point where it emerges from a 1.5km/1mi-long tunnel — the shorter of two tunnels bringing water from a power station near Ribeiro Frio. Almost at once you walk under a spillway protecting the path from the lovely waterfall shown opposite. This part of the levada, where it rounds the head of the **Ribeira de João Gomes**, used to be horrendously vertiginous (see opposite). Now there are railings, but passing other walkers on the narrow path can be a fraught experience!

Eventually you leave this wilderness and come upon a road by the first houses of **Curral dos Romeiros** (**25min**). Turn right downhill, then right again on another road, past the terminus for town bus 29 on the right. This road peters out into a cobbled trail (a continuation of the trail you were on when you left Babosas). A little over ten minutes later, turn left down a narrow path signposted 'Levada do Bom Sucesso' (**1h 05min**). *(Those who avoided the Tornos levada join here.)*

Left: the Levada dos Tornos before the railings were built — people who strayed here by mistake could be paralysed by fear; right: waterfall carrying the João Gomes River into the lower valley

A log-stepped path now takes you very steeply down the east side of the Ribeira de João Gomes, along the 'Green Corridor'. The dark forest of pine and eucalyptus is brightened by a myriad of mimosas and wild flowers in spring. Ten-15 minutes down, a **clearing** makes a pleasant place to pause. It's a good idea to take this opportunity to pack any loose bits away — there's a scramble coming up in a few minutes! Two minutes past the clearing, at a T-junction, the main path goes left. But first go *right,* following red paint lettering on a rock: '**waterfall** 200 m'. You'll quickly see the lovely waterfall shown overleaf, and it's not too difficult to scramble down to the pools in the river bed — a gorgeous place to paddle on a hot day.

Return to the T-junction and now go straight ahead, contouring for a while. Then the stepped path drops very steeply again. Some 10 minutes down from the junction you may be puzzled by a **red arrow** pointing right to a non-existent path. It's there to alert you to a fork a bit further on, where the main path drops steeply to the right and you ignore a level path straight ahead.

After crossing a high, narrow **bridge (1h55min)**, you are finally following the elusive **Levada do Bom Sucesso**, with fantastic views to the expressway, the cable cars and the Bay of Funchal. Ten minutes later a similar **bridge** is crossed; just before it, another red-painted rock alerts you to a

The log-stepped descent to the Bom Sucesso levada. Left: waterfall and pool in the bed of the João Gomes River

waterfall 300 m to the right. *Watch your footing* as you pass below the **expressway (2h10min)**; the path (now below the levada) is very wet and slippery, even in high summer. Keep your mind on the path, although it's tempting to look ahead, to see how many buildings in town you can identify!

All too soon the levada ends, and you meet a T-junction. Walk straight ahead on Rua Dr Antonio Costa (the sign is behind you), past a side-entrance to the **orchid garden** on the left. The road curls right, downhill, to the ER102, where the **bus shelter** is to your left **(2h35min)** and a **bar** to the right.

Londres

We can't even remember when or how we discovered our base restaurant in Funchal; you could walk past and not even notice it. But what we *did* notice, once inside, was that most of the clients were local. Now that it appears in several guides, tourists fill half the seats. Arrive early (before 7.30pm), book ahead, or wait for a table.

Early evening at Londres; later on it will be throbbing!

You can expect value for money, fresh food, fairly unremarkable meat dishes, and *simply superb fresh grilled fish*. The atmosphere is homely, the staff always friendly and helpful, never fussed by the bustle. On arrival you'll be greeted with a plate of marinated broad beans — just perfect with a dry white wine, *vinho verde*, beer or *sercial* aperitif. Whichever meal we are tempted by, we often change our

LONDRES
Rua da Carreira 64A (**291 235 329**
Mon-Sat lunch and dinner €€

daily **main-course specials**; this menu is only printed in Portuguese, so ask them to translate for you; the grilled fresh fish dishes are *highly recommended*.

ten different **entrées**, from the obligatory tomato and onion soup to the exotically translated 'cockles duck style' (see page 28)!

wide range of **omelettes**

meats (usually grilled or fried), including beef (also *espetada*), liver, pork, lamb, chicken, turkey

simple **sweets** and ice creams

minds at the last minute and have the grilled *cherne*, our favourite. A word of warning: one serving is enough for two — especially if you have a first course — and they don't mind if you share.

restaurants

eat

Over the years we've visited many of the restaurants in the capital, including those in the western 'tourist zone'. And you will be very unlucky if you have a bad meal.

One of the most pleasant places to make for is the Old Town, with many excellent restaurants, often with outside tables. Our only complaint there is that some of the busier ones are happy to lure you in, but then even happier to see you go so they can take another seating.

Grilled *cherne* at Londres — each tray holds a serving for one! Below: the Marina Terrace restaurant

We don't like to be rushed (you will *never* be rushed at Londres, no matter how busy).

Another idyllic setting is the marina, with a string of very pleasant settings by the water's edge. If you start at the pier opposite Avenida Zarco and walk west, ignoring the blandishments of all the touts, we'll be surprised if you make it past Fernandes, who will lure

you into the **Marina Terrace**. You won't regret it! The food is superb. Try their tiger prawns or special steak — a very thick fillet served sizzling on a hot stone; they will slice it for you. The menu is huge, with fish and shellfish of all kinds and dishes to appeal to the kids as well — like pastas and pizzas.

MEMORIES OF LONDRES

Broad bean appetizer *(favas)*

You want young (or frozen) broad beans for this dish, or the skins will be too tough. Cook as normally (15-20 minutes), then leave overnight covered in olive oil with some finely chopped onions and parsley (the Londres recipe does *not* call for garlic).

Another popular recipe is for *pickled* broad beans. Make a vinaigrette to the sharpness you like. Add 1 bay leaf, garlic, pepper, allspice and cloves to taste. Store the beans in a large screw-top jar.

'Cockles duck style' *(amêijoas à bulhão pato)*

Served at Londres, this is a very festive-looking dish! Allow about 15 cockles per person, and buy them on the day you will use them. Wash and scrub them clean, then rinse them in 2-3 changes of cold water to remove the grit.

Prepare the rind of one lemon in julienne strips. Steam the cockles for 10 minutes or just until the shells open. (Some may take a minute or two longer, but remove any open cockles from the pan immediately.) *Discard any that do not open.* Pour over melted butter, some garlic juice and lemon juice. Sprinkle the lemon rind and parsley on top.

recipes

eat

There's no point in reproducing Londres' recipe for *cherne*, our favourite meal; it is simply very fresh wreckfish (stone bass), grilled with a bit of crushed garlic and oregano. Instead, here's a recipe for *the* most popular fish dish on the island, *espada com banana*, but with our twist — the bananas are caramelized. If you would find this recipe too sweet, you might prefer to simply fry the bananas in oil or butter — or in *maracujá*, which is how the dish is prepared at O Fio (featured on page 121). Remember, if you make too much, that cold left-over *espada* makes delicious sandwiches!

Espada with bananas (*espada com banana*)

First prepare any vegetables you are having with the meal, since the fish and bananas cook very quickly. Season the fillets with the salt, pepper, garlic and lemon juice. Dust with flour, dip in egg, then coat with breadcrumbs or ground almonds. Halve the bananas lengthwise.

For the fish, coat a suitably sized frying pan with 5mm/1/4" oil and bring to heat. In a separate pan, gently heat the sugar and butter until just bubbling.

Fry the fillets gently for just over two minutes each side, until golden brown. When turning the fish, place the bananas in the caramelized butter; the bananas will only take about two minutes to cook, and both should be just right at the same time. Serve at once!

Ingredients (for 4 people)
400 g *espada* fillets
4 small or Madeiran bananas
1 egg, beaten
salt, freshly ground pepper
1 clove of garlic, crushed
juice of one lemon
1 tbsp sugar
2 tbsp butter
breadcrumbs or ground almonds
flour for dusting
oil for frying

Inaugurated in 1966, the Levada dos Tornos is Madeira's most important levada, with 106km (66mi) of main channels. This walk explores the levada in the primeval João Gomes Valley and then follows an easy stretch — past a lovely tea house — to Palheiro Ferreiro, where you can visit the splendid gardens (with café).

levada dos tornos

WALK

2

To **start the walk**, follow the notes for Walk 1 on page 21 and read the description of the levada path in the upper João Gomes Valley (with photograph on page 23). Then take care to make your decision at the fork reached in **7min**. Will you try the exciting but possibly vertiginous route, or opt for the main trail? If you choose the main trail, just follow it down to the river and back up to the first village en route, where you pick up the notes in the next paragraph.

Whichever route you take, the first habitation you reach is the village of **Curral dos Romeiros** (**25min**). *If you came on the higher levada path,* you will cross a road. Descend steps on the far side, turn left at the bottom, walk past a couple of houses and then go left up steps signed 'Levada dos Tornos/Camacha'. *If you came by the trail with street lights,* just watch for steps on the left marked 'Levada'.

At the top of the steps turn right. You are on the levada but,

Distance: 7.5km/4.6mi; 2h10min

Grade: easy, with an initial ascent of only 90m/300ft. The first part of the walk, in the upper João Gomes Valley, demands a head for heights, but this section can be omitted; see notes at the 7min-point.

Equipment: stout lace-up shoes or walking boots, warm clothing in cool weather, sunhat

Transport: 🚡 cable car (see page 17) or town 🚌 22 to Babosas. Return from Palheiro Ferreiro on town 🚌 36 or 37. (Or end the walk at the Hortensia Tea house and return on town 🚌 47.)

Refreshments en route:
Quinta do Monte (see page 19) or café at one of the cable car stations (all three at the start of the walk)
Hortensia Tea House (1h30min)
Palheiro Ferreiro (at the end)

Points of interest:
Babosas balcony viewpoint
Levada dos Tornos
Palheiro Gardens; Mon-Fri ex holidays, 09.30-16.30 (291 793 044

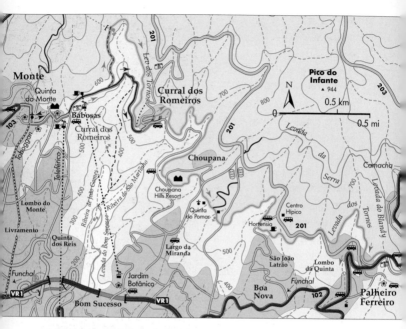

as in all villages, it is covered with concrete slabs. Soon you'll see the watercourse in full flow. Now follow the meandering levada through groves of pine and mimosa, then the beautifully landscaped grounds of the **Choupana Hills Resort Hotel** (**50min**), where you are asked to keep to the path.

On meeting a crossing road (which leads south to the Jardim Botânico; **1h05min**), go through the doorway opposite (sign: 'Levada dos Tornos'). A chapel is on your right; it belongs to the fenced off **Quinta do Pomar** just below the levada. Then you pass a pretty **waterhouse** and a water tank and cross another road.

In about **1h30min** you cross a road by a stop for town bus 47. Some 200m/yds further on, more steps lead up left to the **Hortensia Tea House**, in beautifully land-scaped gardens. Stop to admire the plantings and take some refreshment; if you're in time for lunch, be sure to try some of their delicious home-made vegetable soup.

You cross the ER201 (**1h40min**) and 20 minutes later you reach the ER102. Approach *carefully* — traffic roars round the blind bend to the left. Turn right on the busy road. The entrance to the **Palheiro Gardens** (**2h10min**) is several minutes further downhill, on the left, almost opposite the ER201 to Terreiro da Luta (and another bus stop).

Water for the Levada dos Tornos is collected from three main sources in the north. It runs in open channels to a power station near Ribeiro Frio and from there flows through a very long tunnel (there are 16km/10mi of tunnels on the Tornos!) to the south of the island, emerging into the open again high in the João Gomes Valley — where we meet it on Walks 1 and 2. From there it meanders on to irrigate more than 100,000 outlets between Funchal and Santa Cruz.

The exquisite Palheiro Gardens

Below the main house (privately owned and closed to the public) gentle terraces yield up ever-changing vistas of the formal and informal landscaping, avenues and gardens surrounding the Count of Carvalhal's original *quinta* (now a five-star hotel) and chapel. Your final chance for refreshment is the snack bar/restaurant here (shared with the golfers), before you make your way to the nearest **bus stop**.

Hortensia Tea House

You're really spoilt for choice on this walk, with three watering holes at the start (including the lovely Quinta do Monte) and this charming tea house reached after about 1h30min. At Hortensia you can enjoy home cooking in an intimate, homely setting, with tables indoors and out. The soups are especially recommended on cool winter days — to say nothing of the *poncha!*

HORTENSIA GARDENS
daily except Sundays and Christmas Day, from 10.00-18.00

special 'tea for two' €

salads, **vegetable soups**, **drinks** including non-alcoholic beer, *poncha* (local punch made from lemons, sugarcane spirit and sugar); sandwiches on **home-made bread**, **waffles** with home-made jam, **apple tart** with cream, **scones** (allow 15 minutes)

restaurant

eat

35

'REID'S' CAKE

'The' place to have tea on Madeira is, of course, Reid's Hotel. We used stay there on holiday. One day the hall porter suggested that we go out for a walk — and that was the spark that ignited Sunflower Books years later.

We returned to Madeira once or twice a year for almost a decade, until we had enough material to publish the first edition of *Landscapes of Madeira*. We loved the fruit cake served at tea but, once bitten by the hiking bug, we were never there for tea any more! So on each visit the hall porter always greeted us on arrival with a *whole* rich fruit cake. We called it 'Reid's' Cake'.

Wrapped in brown paper, this could be kept in our room without spoiling for up to three weeks! We had 'tea' on the levadas, always with a slice of that magnificent cake, the perfect hikers' fuel. (*Note:* Please don't call at Reid's and ask to buy one of these cakes; they are just served sliced as one of the cake options with a copious Reid's tea. They only gave us a whole cake because we were very good customers for many years and were out hiking all day, so never there for tea.)

The days when we could afford to spend a month at Reid's are long past, but we do have a brilliant rich fruit cake recipe (see credit on page 140) and always make it at home, then take it to Madeira.

Nowadays there are lovely places all around the island to have tea. Apart from the Hortensia and the Jasmin, one of the best is O Fio at Ponta do Pargo (see pages 121-123), where the herbs for their tisane are grown in pots on the front terrace.

recipes

eat

'Reid's' Cake

Preheat the oven to 180°C, 350°F, gas mark 4.

Grease a 900 g (2 lb) bread loaf tin and line it with non-stick foil (including the corners). Make sure the foil is smooth.

In a large bowl, mix together the flour, sugar, dried fruit, cherries, nuts and mixed spice.

Add the remaining, liquid ingredients and beat the mixture until everything is thoroughly mixed.

Using a flexible spatula, place the mixture in the prepared tin, smooth the surface with a wet knife, and bake in the preheated oven for two hours — or until a skewer inserted into the middle of the cake comes out clean.

Allow to cool completely before removing from the tin. The cake will keep for weeks if wrapped in foil or brown paper and stored in a cool, dry place.

Ingredients (for about 12 servings)

300 g self-raising flour*
300 g granulated sugar*
700 g mixed dried fruit
75 g glacé cherries, chopped
50 g mixed nuts, chopped
1 tsp mixed spice
3 medium eggs, beaten
2 tbsp vegetable oil
250 ml water
1 tbsp black treacle or molasses

*see page 140 for notes about g-f, d-f substitutions

Until the 1950s the post (with vital funds sent home by emigrants) was carried from Funchal to Curral by a woman. Climbing and descending via the Eira do Serrado, with her precious deliveries balanced in a basket on her head, she counted 52 hairpin bends each way. This walk follows the easiest part of her daily round.

curral das freiras

WALK

Start out at the **Eira do Serrado** car park. First climb the aloe-fringed path at the left of the beautifully-situated hotel; it leads to the famous viewpoint, from where you'll enjoy the view shown overleaf — although the landscape still bears the scars of the devastating forest fire of August 2010.

Then return and descend the steps at the right of the sign 'Eira do Serrado Alt. 1094 m' (**15min**). The steps lead into a beautiful old cobbled trail below chestnut trees. Sweet chestnut (*Castanea sativa*) groves have been cultivated on the island since the earliest days of settlement. Not only did the fruit provide food for the population, but the wood had many uses (you'll see a lot of vines in this area on chestnut-wood trellises).

Distance: 3.3km/2mi; 1h30min

Grade: moderate descent of 450m/ 1475ft. In autumn and winter fallen chestnut leaves obscure the path, so watch your footing. Short ascent.

Equipment: stout lace-up shoes or walking boots, warm clothing in cool weather, sunhat

Transport: 🚌 81 or 🚕 to the Eira do Serrado (Mon-Fri 09.00, 10.00, 11.00; Sat 08.45, 10.00, 11.30; Sun 09.05, 11.40). Frequent 81 buses back to Funchal, but only two back to the Eira (14.30 daily; also 16.15 Mon-Fri).

Refreshments en route:
Estalagem Eira do Serrado (at the start)
Vale das Freiras (at the end)

Points of interest:
Eira do Serrado viewpoint
Curral das Freiras
chestnuts!

You clear the trees five minutes down, to be greeted by more superb views — and down here you won't have to share them! As the trail makes a V-turn to the left, you are just level with the entrance to the old road tunnel under the Eira ('Antiga 107', currently closed on account of rock-fall — the locals are

Pico Grande from the Eira do Serrado viewpoint

pressing for it to be re-opened). In contrast to the tunnels built early in the 21st century with massive boring machines financed by the EU, this tunnel (opened in 1959) was man-made — hacked out of the rock with picks. (It is ironic to note that road construction workers are still regularly killed on the island today, despite the plethora of EU health and safety regulations.)

On the far side of the Ribeira do Curral, the houses of Casas Próximas teeter on the *lombo* plunging off Pico do Serradinho. S-bends take you past a couple of well-placed promontories, one of them with an electricity pylon (**45min**). From here there is a view back left to Pico Grande, John's favourite mountain. Contrast this view with the one seen from the Folhadal walk (Walk 10). Pico Grande is easily recognisable from many parts of the island because of the prominent protrusion at the summit.

Beyond this promontory the path, narrow in places, continues to drop sharply in more S-bends. In summer the surrounding cliffs are bright with yellow-flowering houseleeks.

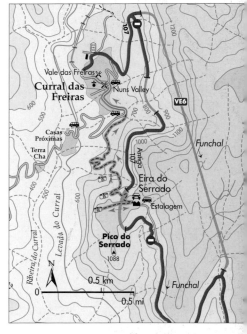

Soon you're just opposite Curral's church, in the setting shown on page 38, and eventually concrete steps take you down to the road (**1h15min**). You could turn left downhill to the nearest bus stop (5min). But we'd suggest you walk 800m uphill (15min) to the Vale das Freiras restaurant in **Curral das Freiras** (**1h30min**). It's on your right, almost opposite the church — a great place to enjoy some roasted chestnuts, chestnut soup and chestnut cake! Then retrace your steps under 200m/yds to the bus stop opposite the Nuns Valley restaurant.

Whether or not you like chestnuts, this walk has two splendid opportunities for a light snack or a very substantial meal. Evening buses back from Curral would even allow you to have an early dinner. (Better still, spend a night at the Estalagem Eira do Serrado and treat yourself!) If you *do* like chestnuts, Curral is nirvana!

Vale das Freiras

This long-established restaurant, a favourite with walkers, has recently doubled in size, with a huge open fire where you can watch your chicken or steak being grilled. Or you may prefer to eat on one

VALE DAS FREIRAS
Curral das Freiras (**291 712 548**
daily, all day €

wide variety of **salads** (including octopus) and **omelettes**

pasta spirals and spaghetti

meats: beef (including *espetada*), pork chops, chicken — grilled on an open fire

fish (cod, sardines, *espada*, octopus), mixed **shellfish** *paella*

chestnut specialities: soup, salad, omelette, cake, liqueurs

of the terraces, with views up to the Eira and surrounding mountains. The portions are hearty, and the food is delicious. Every guest is offered a free home-made liqueur to sample; they have a very large selection — including, of course, chestnut!

restaurants

eat

Estalagem Eira do Serrado

If you love mountains then, without doubt, this hotel has the best views on the island. Breakfast on the terrace of your superbly-appointed room, before the crowds arrive, is unforgettable. But

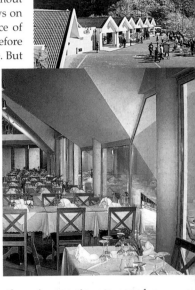

ESTALAGEM EIRA DO SERRADO
Eira do Serrado (291 710 060
www.eiradoserrado.com
daily, all day €–€€

huge menu, with 20 different **entrées**, steaks, chicken, pork, fish and shellfish — all grilled or sauced.

regional specialities *available most Sundays or on special order (telephone two days in advance):* lamb, roast suckling pig, rabbit casserole, roast goat, stuffed turkey, and *cozido* (pork and vegetable stew)

wide variety of **sweets**; chestnut specialities and liqueurs

bar with snacks, chestnut cake, etc

if you've no time to spend a night here, then *do* come for a meal. The dining room sits at the edge of the cliff, with magnificent plummeting views into Curral. Remember that if you come for Sunday lunch, you should be able to choose one of the regional specialities without having to order two days in advance. *A must!*

OVERDOSE ON CHESTNUTS!

Chestnut soup *(sopa de castanha)*

Unless you are using prepared chestnuts, first see notes in the first paragraph of the recipe opposite. In a heavy-bottomed saucepan, heat the oil, toss in the bacon bits and onion, and fry gently until golden.

Add all the other ingredients and bring to the boil. Reduce the heat and simmer for about an hour, or until the vegetables are soft. Serve topped with the parsley.

Roasted chestnuts and chestnut soup at the Vale das Freiras

Ingredients (for 4 people)
1.5 l vegetable stock or bouillon
1 cup of fresh or packaged chestnuts
0.5 kg potatoes, cut in pieces
2 medium sweet potatoes, cut in pieces
2 medium carrots, quite thickly sliced
1 medium onion, chopped
4 tbsp bacon bits ('lardons')
2 tbsp oil
fresh flat parsley
salt and pepper to taste

recipes
eat

Chestnut cake
(bolo de castanha)

If you are using dried chestnuts, soak them overnight and cook until tender (about an hour). If using fresh, boil them for a few minutes, skin them, then boil for about another 20 minutes.

Preheat the oven to 160°C, 325°F, gas mark 3. Prepare a loose-bottomed 20 cm/8 " circular cake tin by greasing thoroughly.

Cream the chestnuts in a blender (if you don't have one, mash them very finely with whatever is to hand!). In a separate container, beat the egg yolks and sugar; add the baking powder and vanilla. Add this mixture to the chestnut purée.

Beat the egg whites until they form soft peaks, then gently fold into the cake mixture.

Cook the cake in the preheated oven for 35min, or until a skewer inserted into the middle comes out clean.

Ingredients (for 10 servings)
300 g fresh or prepared
  chestnuts
125 g granulated sugar
4 eggs, separated
1 tsp baking powder
1 tsp vanilla

Camacha is the centre of the island's wickerwork industry; Santo da Serra is known for its many fine *quintas*. The Levada da Serra (easy strolling) lies above both villages, and the Levada dos Tornos (fairly vertiginous) below. Why not set two days aside to enjoy both routes?

camacha and santo da serra
WALK

Walk 1 introduced the Levada dos Tornos in no uncertain terms! You can follow another stretch of this gorgeous water-course beginning at Camacha and ending at Santo da Serra. But this time there are no railings, and some sections are vertiginous. We hope you *can* manage it, because it is a beautiful walk, and far less visited than the section followed in Walk 2.

But another levada runs not far above these two hill villages. It doesn't carry water any longer (its flow has all been diverted to the Tornos 200m/650ft below). Today it is just a wide trail shaded by mature forest and brightened in summer by a blaze of hydrangeas and agapanthus. This is the Levada da Serra, one of the first to be built on the island.

The ideal way to do this walk would be to take the

On the Tornos (see page 48)

Distance: 16km/10mi; 4h45min

Grade: Easy, but fairly long. You *must be sure-footed and have a head for heights.* You may have to walk *through ice-cold (seasonal) waterfalls.* Short ascent at the end.

Equipment: stout shoes (walking boots preferable), sunhat, plenty of water, snacks, warm clothing all year round, long trousers, whistle, **torch**

Transport: 🚌 129 or 77 to Cama-cha; 🚌 77 from Santo da Serra

Refreshments: restaurants and cafés in Camacha and Santo da Serra; *nothing en route*

Points of interest:
wickerwork at Camacha
quintas at Santo da Serra
the levada and its surroundings

On the Serra (see page 51)

Distance: 17.5km/11mi; 5h

Grade: easy, after an initial climb of 150m/490ft, although quite long

Equipment: as above, but stout shoes will suffice; no torch needed

Transport, refreshments, points of interest: as above *(but to avoid 1h of road-walking, start at Águas Mansas; see footnote page 51)*

47

Palm tree shortly after joining the
Levada dos Tornos

Tornos from Camacha to
Santo da Serra and, another
day, the Serra back to
Camacha (where you could
stock up on wickerwork!).

Both routes start in
Camacha's main square (the
Achada da Camacha). First
take a peep at the magnificent
wickerwork in the Café/
Estalagem do Relógio. When
you leave the shop, the Tornos
route lies in the south and the
Serra route (description overleaf) to the north.

For the Tornos route:
Facing the Café do Relógio, descend the road on the right (signposted to Funchal), passing the new village church on your left.
Ignore a small road off right, cross the bypass road and continue
down the steep road almost opposite (Caminho Fonte Conce-
los). In **7min** fork right, then look left for a fine view over the
Porto Novo Valley. A few minutes later, at a T-junction, turn left.
Now watch for where this road crosses the **Levada dos Tornos**
(by a small parking bay; **14min**) and turn left on the levada.

Before long (**23min**) you pass a house with the magnificent
palm tree shown above; a road runs along on the right here.
Keep up on the levada, and you will come to a **tunnel** a minute

Notes for this route continue on page 53

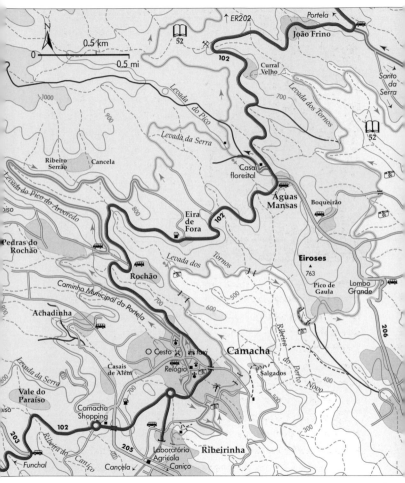

For the Serra route:*
With your back to the
Café do Relógio, cross
the square and walk
north uphill on the road
signposted to Santo da
Serra. You pass the res-
taurants 'O Cesto' on
the left and 'O Boléu'
on the right (see page
56). Then climb the

Hydrangeas (above) and oaks (left) flank the
dry Levada da Serra

narrow road just north of Camacha's old church (the Camiñho
Municipal da Portela, with walkers' signposts on the left).

When you reach the crossing **Levada da Serra** (under
15min), turn right and just stride out (or stroll along),
eventually crossing the road to Poiso and Pico do Arieiro
(ER202; about **3h**). Some 1h15min later you cross a track and
come to the **Santo da Serra waterhouse** (**4h15min**). Enjoy its
shady pines and charming gardens, then return to the track and
descend to the ER102 (25min). Turn right downhill, then turn
left into **Santo da Serra** (20min; **5h**). Restaurante Casa do
Campo (see page 57) is on your right, in a mini 'commercial
centre', not far past the petrol station.

*This levada has been covered by a road in the Porto Novo Valley (3km). To
avoid asphalt and save about 1h30min, take 🚐 77 to Águas Mansas. From the
junction of the ER206 and the ER102, walk 100m/yds north towards Santo da
Serra, then turn left up a road. Past a forestry house, the road reverts to track.
Keep left at a fork, then fork right uphill on a path beside the rushing Levada do
Pico. When you reach the (dry) Levada da Serra in 10 minutes, turn right.

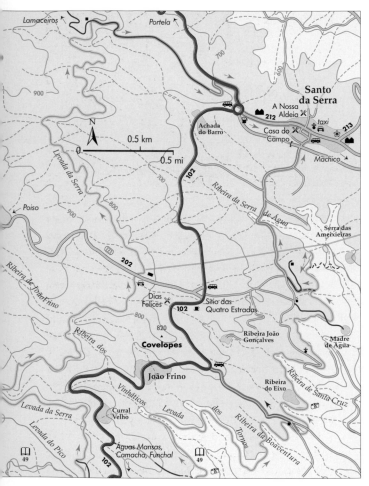

Terraces, hidden glens of cala lilies, pools and
waterfalls in the lower Porto Novo Valley

Tornos route (continued from page 48)

later, where you will need your torch for three minutes. Another
tunnel is met in **40min** (two minutes; no torch needed). Beyond
this tunnel there is a possibility of vertigo: although the path is
very adequate, there is *no* protective fencing, and the drops are
severe — perhaps 50m/150ft. Often ice-cold waterfalls cascade
onto the path as well, and you may get soaked. Watch out, too,
for the concrete blocks in the path, supporting the pipe carrying
some of the water. But this part of the walk, in the lower part of
the **Ribeira do Porto Novo**, is one of the most beautiful
stretches of the Tornos. Suddenly birds and cascades are singing
everywhere. In **50min** the levada makes a U-turn high in the
valley, below some pools. The waterfall shown above crashes
into the river; all else is stillness. This is an idyllic rest spot.

Go through the third and shortest **tunnel** (**1h**), then skirt
round a **tunnel with 'windows'** (**1h10min**). *Be sure to climb up
steps beyond this tunnel to rejoin the Tornos; the levada ahead runs*

53

Boaventura Valley in early autumn

down to Gaula. Soon you reach a reservoir at **Lombo Grande** (**1h30min**) and then the ER206. If you need an 'escape route', turn right and descend for a minute to a bus stop, where bus 60 leaves for Funchal at noon (not Sundays).

Crossing straight over the road, in under ten minutes you have good views over the airport and São Lourenço Point. After 20 minutes you pass through a very short **tunnel** (no torch is needed, but it is very low: watch your head!) and come out in the **Ribeira da Boaventura**. While the Porto Novo is our favourite part of the Tornos in spring, in summer the Boaventura Valley takes the prize. The terraces are golden with wheat, and the levada paths are aglow with blue and white agapanthus — so tall and thick that they are almost like hedgerows. You progress quite easily for a good 20 minutes past the tunnel, but then the way becomes vertiginous, as it delves into a very deep tributary, the **Ribeira dos Vinháticos**. By **2h20min** you reach the head of this stream. The next, smaller tributary, is a basin full of willow.

In just over **3h05min** you pass a waterhouse on the left; beyond it is a road. Two minutes later a second road is crossed (**3h10min**). Both lead up to the ER102 at João Frino, if you're pressed for time and trying to catch bus 77. Beyond the second road you delve into the upper reaches of a new valley — the

Ribeira de Santa Cruz. Ignore all the cobbled trails and paths crossing the levada during the next 45 minutes or so; civilisation seems very far away, as you enter an emerald wilderness.

Then suddenly, at **3h55min**, the levada ends. Unbelievable! How can this magnificent watercourse, which has carried you through the most beautiful valleys in the southeast, have abandoned you without warning? Its waters shoot out into a tank some 200m/650ft below, to feed the Levada Nova. A **pipe** coming in from the Levada da Serra runs down and over to the *lagoa* (reservoir) above Santo da Serra.

Walk back along the levada for six minutes, then turn right up cobbled steps. A few minutes uphill, you emerge in fields. Head towards the electricity wires in front of you, keeping to the left of the plots. At a stone wall, bear left. Bear left again at a second wall, quickly coming to a cobbled track. Go left uphill (past the entrance to a *quinta*), to an asphalted crossroads.

Turn right here and follow the Caminho da Pereira, for the final stretch into Santo da Serra. You first skirt the grounds of this mysterious *quinta,* overgrown with luxuriant vegetation. For a short time in the 1800s it was home to a young Scottish doctor, Robert Reid Kalley, esteemed by the islanders for his near-miraculous cures. But he was also a Protestant, and when the authorities would no longer tolerate his incessant proselytising, he had to flee dressed as a woman.

The road crosses the **Ribeira da Serra de Água** and eventually rises through housing. When you emerge at **Santo da Serra (4h45min)**, the restaurant Casa do Campo (see page 57) is just to your left, on the left-hand side of the road.

O Cesto

You can get a drink or snack in the bar here from 10am to 10pm, but the restaurant is only open for lunch (from 12.00 to 16.00). The meals, served in a very comfortable, large dining room, are delicious (see next pages for two of their specialities), and the wine list more than adequate.

Almost opposite is **O Boléu**, also serving home-cooked fare (especially delicious soups). Both restaurants serve the excellent local bread.

O CESTO
Camacha (just south of the old church) (291 922 068
bar daily 10.00-22.00 €
restaurant daily except Thur 12.00-16.00 €

bar for light snacks, including tongue, *espada*, steak sandwiches

restaurant serving substantial home-cooked fare with Madeiran/Portuguese specialities including *carne de vinho e alhos* and *frango na púcara* (see page 59).

You need never go hungry in Camacha! The **Relógio** in the main square is also an hotel and always open. Its menu (regional and international) is huge. It's a bit pricier than Cesto or Boléu — unless you choose the tasty and economical special *(prato do dia)*.

Fanciful wickerwork on display at the Café/Estalagem do Relógio

restaurants

eat

Casa do Campo

This cheerful and very comfortable restaurant is a real boon to Santo da Serra. The food is delicious, the portions massive (try having soup, then splitting a main course — they won't mind).

Casa do Campo is spotlessly clean — and you can look through the plate glass partition into the kitchen (in the background).

> **CASA DO CAMPO**
> Santo da Serra (291 552 880
> daily from 12.00-23.00 €€; credit
> cards are not accepted!
>
> **soups** or **chicken salad** are the only light dishes; no omelettes or sandwiches
>
> various **pastas** make a change — with meat, vegetarian or fish sauces
>
> **fish and seafood** a speciality, especially octopus (polvo) dishes
>
> interesting variations on the usual Madeiran treatment of **meats**, like chicken curry; also pork and beef
>
> good selection of Continental and Madeiran **wines**

A Nossa Aldeia (€) is a bright pink building on a side-road almost opposite Casa do Campo. It's not as comfortable: seating is on wooden benches at long, shared tables. But the rustic decor and low prices compensate. They do soups, egg dishes and omelettes for a light meal; also *espada, bacalhau* and the usual meats (including tongue in wine sauce), but the locals mostly tuck into *espetada* and *milho frito*.

Should you walk the Serra route (page 51) and decide to call it a day at the ER202, try **Dias Felices** (€), just 150m west of the Sitio das Quatro Estradas. Run by a young couple, this has *no menu*, just one dish of the day (although they will do *espada* or steak on request). Little English is spoken, but the service is virtually instant, the food very good (we could hardly believe that the delicious sauce on John's steak was flour-free), and it is very, *very* inexpensive!

HEARTY HILL-VILLAGE FARE

Meat (pork) with wine and garlic *(carne de vinho e alhos)*

This dish must be prepared a few days in advance. Roll the pork cubes in the salt and refrigerate overnight. Transfer the meat to an

oven-proof casserole, pour over the marinade, cover, and refrigerate for three to four days.

Preheat the oven to 150°C, 300°F, gas mark 2. On top of the stove, bring the meat and marinade just to the boil, then transfer to the oven. Cover and cook for 1h, then allow to cool.

Ingredients (for 4 people)
700 g loin of pork with
    plenty of fat, cut into
    3 cm cubes
coarse salt
lard

For the marinade:
250 ml white wine
100 ml vinegar
black pepper
6 cloves garlic, crushed
1 bay leaf

Skim off the fat and heat in a large frying pan. Fry the meat over a quite high flame, turning, until all sides are golden *(Do not crowd the pan, or the meat will steam. Keep cooked cubes warm in the oven.)* If there is not enough fat, add some lard. If the sauce reduces too much, slowly add more wine.

This dish is traditionally served with boiled *and* sweet potatoes and orange slices. It may also be served with fried bread that has been pre-soaked in the marinade (you would need to *double* the marinade ingredients).

recipes

eat

Chicken in a pot *(frango na púcara)*

Easy to prepare, this O Cesto speciality originated in mainland Portugal. Our recipe is just one of *many* variations; some add *aguardente,* shallots or white wine; others omit the red pepper.

Preheat the oven to 180°C, 350°F, gas mark 4. Fry the chicken pieces in 2 mm oil until golden on all sides. Pat dry on paper towels. Remove to a heavy casserole, add the other ingredients (pre-mixed), and cook, covered, for 40 minutes. Uncover and cook for another 20 minutes, by which time the sauce will have reduced nicely.

Serve with rice or boiled potatoes and vegetables, or with sweet potato bread (see page 92) and a simple salad.

Ingredients (for 4 people)
1 chicken (1.5 kg), jointed
oil of choice (for frying the chicken)
150 ml vegetable stock
100 ml port or madeira wine
1 tin (400 g) chopped tomatoes
1 tsp Dijon mustard
100 g Portuguese sausage *(chouriço),* sliced
2 tbsp diced sweet red pepper
2 cloves garlic, crushed

This is a five-star walk to which we return again and again, to enjoy the wonderful play of light and shade along the Levada do Furado, the limpid pools of the Levada do Bezerro, and the centuries-old trails around Ribeiro Frio — to say nothing of a trout lunch!

around ribeiro frio
WALK

5

Begin the walk just below the **Restaurante Ribeiro Frio**, where you will see a signpost 'PR10, Portela' on your right (further downhill, on the left, is a sign for Balcões, a viewpoint you might like to visit later in the day; see pages 64-65). Following the 'Portela' sign, you join the fast-flowing **Levada do Furado**. While this levada used to be tricky underfoot, recent repairs and new protective railings allow you to appreciate the play of light and shade created by the laurel and heath trees in comfort and safety.

In **20min** you pass a tunnel on the right, where a waterfall feeds the levada. In **1h**, just by a bridge over the **Ribeira do Poço do Bezerro**, two fast-flowing, channelled levadas course down into the main channel at a grassy verge (see photograph overleaf). The finches here have been tamed by decades of walkers using *Landscapes of Madeira*, and will expect to be fed some titbits!

Distance: 7km/4.3mi; 3h

Grade: moderate, with an ascent of 300m/1000ft. *Not suitable in wet weather or heavy mist!*

Equipment: walking boots or stout shoes that grip on slippery surfaces, long trousers, warm clothing all year round, water

Transport: 🚌 56 or 103 to Ribeiro Frio; 🚌 103 to return. Or 🚗. Buses stop at the Ribeiro Frio Restaurant; there is a large souvenir shop (and a bar) opposite

Refreshments en route:
Restaurante Ribeiro Frio (start/end)
Bar Ribeiro Frio (start/end)
Bar Flor da Selva (on the Balcões path; optional extension)

Points of interest:
trout hatchery and small botanical gardens
old trails and farm at Feiteiras
Levada do Furado
source of the Levada do Bezerro

Optional extension:
Balcões (3km/2mi; 50min return): see pages 64-65

Turn right at the finches ...

The walk described in that book continues along the Furado levada and then down to Portela, but for this circuit, you now head uphill to the right. Clamber 2m/6ft up the bank above the *left-hand* channel, to a path. Follow this beside the narrow **Levada do Bezerro**, rising through ferns and greenery in the setting shown opposite. You come to some lovely pools and polished boulders in the **Ribeira do Poço do Bezerro (2h)**, where this levada takes its source.

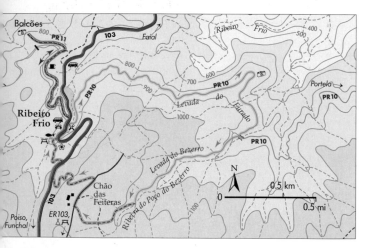

... and follow the narrow Levada do Bezerro up past waterfalls to its source. Then return and climb a sometimes-stepped path to the plateau.

From here retrace your steps for 30m/yds, then turn left up a narrow path (cairn). The path emerges from the trees on a sloping plateau (the **Chão das Feiteiras**). The odd, fairly large cairn marks the route as you follow a trodden path through ferns *(feiteiras)* — at first heading due west (over a crossing path) and then north-northwest. If the weather is clear, there is a brilliant view to the high peaks on this gentle ascent. The path emerges at a clearing by **three farm buildings (2h30min)**.

Turn right in front of the buildings but, after 200m/yds, turn left on a grassy trail, going through a gate after 20m. Soon cobbles come underfoot. Descend to the ER103, cross it, and pick up the continuing trail 200m/yds downhill. When this beautiful old trail again meets the ER103, turn right downhill for a couple of minutes, then pick up the continuation of the

Old trail down to the trout farm (left) and light and shade on the Levada do Furado

trail, on the left. Finally you come upon a beautiful setting, where a levada descends in tiers just above the **trout farm**. Inspect the hatchery (work up an appetite!), take a look at the tiny botanical gardens, then make your way back down to the Restaurante Ribeiro Frio for a late lunch (**3h**). It's quite pricey, but the setting is utterly charming.

If you have time after lunch, take a short walk to one of the island's most spectacular viewpoints — **Balcões** (the balconies); it's just 50min there and back. The wide, signposted path (PR11) is below the souvenir shop and bar. Follow it beside the *dry* Levada do Furado, past a bar/souvenir stall. After passing

Balcões: view over the Fajã da Nogueira Valley and to the high peaks (from left to right: Pico do Arieiro, the pointed needle of Pico do Gato, the jagged spires of Pico das Torres and finally Pico Ruivo and the Achada do Teixeira plateau)

through a cutting in the towering, moss-covered basalt, you find yourself high in the Metade Valley and reach a fork, where the old levada goes left*; turn right and you're at the **Balcões** in a minute. There are superb views over Fajã da Nogueira and to the high peaks. At the power station below, water collected from the north is channelled via the long tunnels of the Levada dos Tornos to the João Gomes Valley, explored on Walk 1.

*Despite the sign here indicating no entry for walkers, you *could* walk along the old levada *for just a short way* (to where a path drops down right to the power station track), but beyond this point it's completely crumbled away.

Restaurante Ribeiro Frio

Originally opened in the early 1980s and called Victor's, this restaurant was one of our favourites. Since then it has become so popular that you may have to wait a long time to be served. Do *not* arrive between 10.00-11.30, when the coaches create absolute havoc! Inside there's a cosy 'snug' bar, as well as the main restaurant (with simple benches). Outside there's a large terrace with sun umbrellas — so, whatever the weather, enjoy the wait in idyllic surroundings!

The trout farm (above) and rustic setting of the Restaurante Ribeiro Frio

RESTAURANTE RIBEIRO FRIO

Ribeiro Frio (**291 575 898 daily 09.30-18.00** €→€€€

trout (from the fish farm) is the speciality — including thick trout soup, and baked, grilled or smoked trout

soups, **omelettes** and **salads** for a light meal

various **pastas**

fish dishes include tuna steak, *espada* with banana (see *our* recipe on page 29), grilled *bacalhau*

meats include mixed grill, steaks, pork, chicken and, surprisingly, **lamb cutlets**

coffee or tea with a good selection of **cakes** and **tarts** from €

restaurants

eat

Trout soup *(sopa de truta)*
Despite the Portuguese name, this recipe comes from the Black Forest (Victor was German).

Cook the trout in 4 cups of cold water with the bay, clove and bouquet garni for about 20 minutes. Then put in a blender (or mash down) and heat till reduced to about 3 cups. Add the cream, salt, pepper. Add 1 tbsp. cold water to the egg yolk to prevent curdling, then add a little hot liquid. Return to the pan (do *not* let it boil) and stir as it thickens.

Place the smoked trout bits in warm soup plates and pour over the hot soup. Sprinkle with the freshly chopped dill.

Lamb cutlets *(costeleta de borrego)*
A popular dish at Easter — a treat, as young lamb does not often figure in the local diet.

Marinate the cutlets in all the other ingredients and refrigerate, covered, overnight. Then grill or barbecue, basting liberally with the marinade. Serve with mashed potato (with garlic and olive oil).

Ingredients (for 4 people)
for the soup:
1 fresh trout, boned,
   skinned, filleted and
   cut into small pieces
1/2 smoked trout fillet,
   cut in slivers
1 bay leaf, 1 clove,
   1 bouquet garni, salt
   and fresh-ground
   pepper
1 egg yolk
2 cups double cream
fresh dill

for the cutlets
8 lamb cutlets
1 clove garlic, crushed
200 ml white wine
100 ml olive oil
2 cloves, 2 bay leaves
fresh chopped parsley
salt and pepper to taste

recipes

eat

This hike takes you high above the sea, across grassy terraces veined with old stone walls, before dropping down to Caniçal on a somewhat precipitous path. After a break (and a short slog up a dirt road), you follow a narrow levada through mimosas and along sunny slopes, before making a dramatic descent to the old main road.

caniçal circuit

WALK

Start out at the **Pico do Facho** bus stop on the west side of the **Caniçal tunnel**. Climb the road towards the peak. Electricity pylons will guide you from here to Caniçal: *take note of them!* The **first pylon** comes up just before the peak: you will leave the road here and walk left on a track (just opposite a narrow trail rising up from Machico). But first walk another five minutes up to **Pico do Facho** (**25min**), for a wonderful view of Machico and its harbour, the airport and São Lourenço Point.

Return to the pylon and, some 10m/yds below it, turn right on a track. At a Y-fork, bear left (the right-hand fork runs to a ramshackle shed). Your left fork immediately becomes a path which runs at the top of some still-cultivated terraces, passes well above the **second pylon**, and takes you straight to the **third pylon**

Distance: 9km/5.6mi; 3h50min

Grade: moderate, with overall ascents/descents of about 300m/ 1000ft; you must be sure-footed and have a head for heights (danger of vertigo).

Equipment: walking boots, sunhat, long-sleeved shirt, long trousers, plenty of water

Transport: 🚌 113 to/from the old Caniçal tunnel on the ER109: alight at the western end and return from the eastern end. 🚗 By car, park well tucked in at the side of the road to Pico do Facho (or park at Caniçal and start the walk there — if you can wait 4-5h to eat!).

Shorter version: do either half of the main walk, ending at or starting from Caniçal (🚌 113). Grade and equipment as above. Allow 1h40min for the first half, 2h for the second.

Refreshments en route:
O Tonel, 350m west of where the walk starts, on the ER109
Restaurants/snack bars in Caniçal (halfway point)

Points of interest:
Pico do Facho viewpoint
whaling museum in Caniçal; 10.00-12.00 and 13.00-18.00; closed Mondays, holidays ✆ 291 961 858

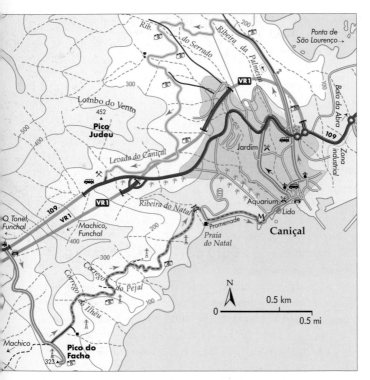

(**50min**). Here, on a ridge between the **Ilhéu** and **Pejal** streams, you enjoy you first views of Caniçal.

Watch out here. The path seems to 'disappear' on bedrock. In fact it unexpectedly turns *inland,* to descend the north side of the ridge. So go *left* up the bedrock and after 20 paces fork right, to continue the descent into the next valley. Soon (**1h**) the **fourth**

pylon is about 150m/yds ahead of you. *Watch out here, too!* Do *not* follow the path towards this pylon. The path you want (not easily seen at first) turns off to the right and runs about 20m/60ft *below* the pylon, rounding it on the sea side *(follow the red paint dots)*, zigzagging and dropping considerably.

Humpback bridge over the Ribeira do Natal

When you come to the next bedrock area at a precipice (**1h10min**), the path bends sharply to the left. You overlook Caniçal here. Ten minutes from this precipice, you pass to the left of the **fifth pylon (1h25min)**, from where the end of the walk is in view. Looking inland, you spot a beautiful old humpback footbridge over the **Natal** stream below. The path takes you down to it — a scramble involving all fours. Once over the **bridge (1h35min)**, take the tarmac road down to the seafront. On the far side of the building (bar, toilets), follow the seafront promenade to the left, past the **whaling museum** in **Caniçal** (as of press date this new museum was still not open — probably due to lack of funds). Just past the **lido** is **Aquarium**, our recommended restaurant (see page

74). Take the next left turn (the third left off the seafront), rising to the **old church** (**1h50min**; bus stop). Head east from the church on the main street*, then take the second left; Caniçal's large, newer church (with a clock) is ahead on the right. Cross straight over the main ER109 road to Baía da Abra; the **'Correos' building** will be on your right (**2h10min**). Climb the road opposite, passing a **water tank** on the right. The asphalt ends at a white-walled **cemetery** on the left. Walk past it on the now unsurfaced road; you'll soon see the levada running in the gutter at the left.

After another 700m/yds, the narrow **Levada do Caniçal** curves left, away from the dirt road (which continues straight on) and enters a **wood** full of mimosas. Soon you pass a **narrower levada** rushing down to the left (**2h40min**). Beyond a crossing track, a grassy verge affords a splendid view back down over Caniçal and to an idyllic pink farmhouse surrounded by its beautifully planted plots, the whole framed by a wreath of yellow mimosas. You're heading into a deep tributary of the **Ribeira do Serrado**. A few minutes later (**3h**), you cross the head of this valley on a levada 'bridge' with protective railings.

Before long the fine buttress of rock formed by the **Lombo do Vento** and **Pico Judeu** rises nearby on your right. An earthen track joins the levada, and you follow it for a short time, leaving the woods behind for the view shown on page 68. Rejoining the

*But to eat at Jardim (see page 74), keep ahead, with the old church on your right. Go right at a Y-fork, to pass Jardim on your right. Later, turn right at the T-junction with the ER109 for 300m, to the 'Correos' building on the left.

Near the end of the walk, the levada runs through tall grasses.

levada, a long sunny stretch takes the ribbon of water through high grasses, with just the odd tree offering welcome shade.

Eventually the watercourse rounds a bend, and now the narrow path runs at the top of a concrete wall high above the ER109 … and below a quarry (**3h45min**). This is a stunning section of the hike. When you come to a concrete track, descend left to the road, where you can *flag down* a bus (**3h50min**). Motorists should turn right and follow the road through the **Caniçal road tunnel** (add 15min; there is a pavement, but this is still very unpleasant — it's almost worth taking a bus to the far side!).

Restaurante Jardim

As is name implies, this restaurant is set in lovely gardens. You can dine indoors (huge windows) or on the outdoor terrace with retractable roof. Beautifully decorated, spotlessly maintained, this is an extremely pleasant atmosphere for enjoying a leisurely meal.

JARDIM
Sítio Palmeira de Baixo, Caniçal (**291 969 120 daily except Mon 10.00-23.00** €–€€

large selection of **entrées**, specialising in all kinds of shellfish, octopus, etc

soups and **omelettes** for a lighter meal

fish dishes include tuna steak, *espada* (fillets or on the bone), sautéed octopus with chips, *bacalhau*, creamed mixed shellfish

meats steak with mushrooms, pork cutlets, *picado* (sautéed meat and chips)

basic **sweets** — including the ubiquitous velvet *pudim* and chocolate mousse

reasonable **wine list**, mostly Alentejos

Jardim, with views to the outdoor terrace

There are also several new restaurants on the front — such is the rapid growth of Caniçal since the opening of the *zona industrial*. We highly recommend **Aquarium** (see opposite). **O Tonel**, 350 m west of the Pico do Facho road (open daily 10.00-22.00, (291 962 459), has been around since time immemorial and serves very standard Madeiran fare in an old-fashioned setting.

restaurants

eat

Aquarium

This new restaurant is very popular with the locals — and deservedly so. The food is good, the menu is wide-ranging, and it's incredibly cheap ('dish of the day' — for instance roast chicken or tuna steak, with coffee, for 5 €). Plan to arrive early for lunch or be prepared to wait — not only to be served, but perhaps just to get a table. You'll pass Aquarium on the seafront, just before turning uphill to the old church to continue the walk.

Among the chef's specialities is *espada* roe (*ovas*), which we've never seen on any other menus. Another is *arroz de marisco* (rice with shellfish), one of Pat's favourites — a real treat with crispy bread and a salad. Of course they serve grilled limpets (everyone does), *but* this is the only place we've been able to enjoy grilled mussels.

> **AQUARIUM**
> **Serrado da Igreja, Caniçal**
> (291 628 154
> **daily 09.00-23.00 €**
>
> wide range of fish- and seafood-based **entrées**, with some dishes not seen elsewhere on the island
>
> **soups**, **omelettes** and **salads** for a lighter meal
>
> varied **fish** dishes, not just the usual tuna and *espada*, but wrasse, grouper, gillhead bream
>
> **meats** are fairly standard — steak, pork, *picado* (sautéed meat and chips)
>
> for **sweets** there's nothing special, but they do have fruit pies and ice-creams
>
> only a couple of basic **wines**, but plenty of local and international alcoholic drinks and **beers** (bottled or on tap); fresh **juices**

This easy (but quite long) walk in the Serra das Funduras takes you through an area where the ancient *laurisilva* forest is being regenerated with the help of EU funding. You'll walk among not only laurels, but *folhados* (see Walk 10), myrtles and tree ferns.

serra das funduras

WALK

Begin the walk at **Portela**: head east on the narrow road skirting the north side of the restaurant **Miradouro da Portela**. There may be a 'PR5' information board here. The narrow **Levada da Portela** runs along on your right. When the tarred road swings right (to Ribeira de Machico), keep ahead on an earthen track. After 200m/yds you pass an old trail down left to Porto da Cruz. In the 1800s the *borracheiros* used this trail to transport wine, carried in goatskins, from Porto da Cruz to the south. There are magnificent views down over 'Eagle Rock' and the north coast … *if* the weather is fine.

Distance: 16km/10mi; 3h55min

Grade: easy, but quite long (ample opportunities to shorten the walk; see the map on page 79). If the weather is poor, keep to the footpaths; the tracks are quite boring, unless the views are fine! Some of the paths are narrow and slippery; you must be sure-footed.

Equipment: stout shoes, warm clothing all year round, sunhat, plenty of water and snacks

Transport: 🚌 53 or 78 to/from Portela, or by 🚗

Refreshments en route:
Bar/Restaurant Miradouro da Portela at the viewpoint; *recommended*
Bar Portela a Vista, below the pass on the Machico road

Points of interest:
laurisilva forest (under protection)
views to Penha de Águia and over the north coast

At a fork (**20min**), keep left (Portela's transmitter mast is up to the right). Six-seven minutes later, be sure to turn right on the first of the three footpaths created in the forest; this one is 2.5km long. (There should be an **information panel or PR5 fingerpost** here, but it may be missing.) While dense foliage obscures most of the views, there are occasional glimpses of the Machico Valley and the golf course at Santo da Serra. The path undulates

In the *laurisilva* (left) and steps opposite the forestry house

along the contours, just on the leeward side of the ridge.

Eventually steps on the left take you back to the track (**1h10min**). Turn right and come almost at once to another **signboard**. On the left are picnic tables and the second footpath. We will return by that path; for now, follow the track downhill to the right. Three minutes later, at a junction, go left. In another seven minutes, go left again at another junction, descending slightly. You round the huge basin of the **Ribeira das Cales**. At a fork, keep left uphill, to the **Casa das Funduras** (forestry

house and more picnic tables), opened in 2002 (**1h45min**). From here the PR5 descends to Maroços; we do *not*.

Leaving the forestry house off to the right, stay on the track which curls left. *Ignore* a path on the right 200m/yds along but, 25m further on, fork right on the third sign-posted footpath (1km). When it ends, more steps take you up left to another picnic area and **viewpoint** (**1h55min**), from where Pico do Facho is seen. From here go left along the track, passing the EU-sponsors' signboard on your left.

Back at the forestry house (**2h 05min**), climb the path on your right. This rises above the track, with fine views to conical **Pico Coroa** at the head of the valley. This path (also 2.5km) is perhaps the prettiest of all, dotted with fern trees.

Restaurante Miradouro da Portela (the original cottage has the thatched roof) and the deep wood fire in the snug, where *espetada* sizzles

When you meet the track again (**2h45min**) go right, uphill (or, if visibility is poor, keep to the prettier path). Once over a rise, 15 minutes along the track, you regain fine views over the north coast. Follow the track all the way back to **Portela** (**3h55min**). We do hope you've worked up an appetite!

Miradouro da Portela

We'll never forget our first meal here. We'd been walking the Levada do Furado (see Walk 5) from Ribeiro Frio to Portela on a cold, miserable day. Our only sustenance was some 'Reid's Cake' (see page 36-37) which we'd scoffed in the shelter of rock overhangs. Eventually descending to Portela in drizzle, a thatched cottage (as it was then) loomed ahead in the fog. Inside was a rip-roaring fire. Bliss!

MIRADOURO DA PORTELA
Portela (291 966 169
daily 09.30-22.00 €

espetada is the speciality, but there are **soups** and **omelettes**, including parsley *(salsa)* omelette, for a lighter meal

We were famished. They suggested their 'usual' menu, which turned out to be the marathon meal described on the next two pages! Luckily we had until early evening to catch the last bus back to Funchal. It was delicious — one of the most memorable meals we've ever had on the island.

Now, forewarned, we only order *one espetada* for two people (pictured above is *one* serving — 6 large cubes). The wood fire is so hot that *espetada* of fillet (this is the *only* restaurant we know that offers a *choice of beef*) cooks in three minutes. With a bottle of red Monte Velho, it is superb. They *do* have a large restaurant room, but we always opt for the cosy snug, with its hard wooden benches.

restaurants

eat

THE 'WHOLE WORKS'

Tomato soup (*sopa de tomate*)

Simmer the tomatoes, potatoes and onion together in the oil for 15 minutes or so, until very soft. (If you use tinned tomatoes, you'll need *three* 400 g tins to retain enough liquid.) Then purée (or sieve); season to taste. Serve with a poached egg on top. (See photograph on page 92, which shows this soup in a different style — the onions have not been puréed; at the Miradouro da Portela they *are*.)

Flat bread (*bolo do caco*)

Mix all the ingredients together, using enough water to make a light, puffy dough. Allow to rise, then knead well on a floured board until it has an elastic consistency. Cover and leave to rise for another hour.

Divide and mould into four circles. Unless you have a wood-burning oven (in which case cook them on a hot stone), fry like pancakes on a very hot non-stick griddle, turning after they have spread to about 3 cm thick and the first side has a fine crust. Serve hot with butter or garlic butter. (See photograph on page 7.)

Whimsical outdoor barbecues are very popular!

<u>Ingredients (for 4 people)</u>

for the soup:
1 kg tomatoes, peeled and
   chopped
2 small onions, finely chopped
2 medium potatoes, cubed
garlic juice to taste (optional)
4 eggs
2 tbsp olive oil
salt and pepper

for the bread
1 kg plain flour
1 kg puréed sweet potatoes,
   cooled
25 g yeast
warm salted water as needed
salt to taste

recipes

eat

Beef on a skewer (*espetada*)

Roll the beef cubes in the crushed garlic and salt and let it 'rest' for half an hour. Put on skewers or laurel branches, inserting a fresh laurel (bay) leaf between each cube. Cook over a hot fire, preferably with some laurel twigs in the wood or charcoal. In this photo, taken at our barbecue in Funchal, the potatoes (in foil) baked in 30 minutes; the (fillet) of beef was done (rare) in 10 minutes.

'Oven chips'

Preheat the oven to 180°C, 350°F, gas mark 4. Chop the potatoes into 3 cm cubes and boil in salted water for 5 minutes, then drain well and dry off in the warm cooking pan for another 5 minutes.

Transfer to an oven pan lightly coated with olive oil. Sprinkle with a little coarse salt and some finely-crushed dry laurel leaves. Toss the lot together with wooden spoons and roast, turning a couple of times, for 30 about minutes.

Ingredients (for 4 people)

1 kg of sirloin or fillet steak, cut into 5 cm cubes (if you are using a tougher cut of beef, first marinate it in white wine for 24 hours)
6 garlic cloves, crushed
coarse salt (to taste)
laurel twigs and plenty of fresh bay leaves
4 large potatoes (if baking), or 8 medium potatoes, peeled (if making 'oven chips')
olive oil
salad makings, salad dressing

An old zigzag trail, high cliffs, the throbbing sea beside you … this walk was made in heaven. The ideal way to do it is to take bus 56 or 103 to *Santana*, see the village, then *walk* 2km to the Quinta do Furão for lunch (at 12 sharp!). Unless you have a car, end at São Jorge or take the short-cut path to the Vigia, to catch the last bus!

santana and são jorge

WALK

View east to the Achada do Gramacho and the Ilh...

To start the walk, climb the road on the north side of the 'Solar' bus stop, passing flower-filled gardens. In 4min you come to a rosy-pink *solar*, now in ruins. These early manors were the homes of sugar-mill and plantation owners. Fork right in front of the façade, curving below the building on a track (initially concreted), overlooking the Achada do Gramacho, a small plain laced with vines.

On reaching a road at the Quinta do Furão, turn right. Just before the entrance to the restaurant, head up left past a viewpoint to some wooden fencing which guides you round the north side of the hotel and a conical hill, the Cabeço da Vigia. When the fencing ends, keep along the edge of the cliffs on a narrow path. As the path dives down right, take steps up left to a turning circle. Follow the road

Distance: 10.5km/6.5mi; 3h30min

Grade: moderate-strenuous, with over 400m/1300ft of descents/ ascents. *Not recommended in damp weather, when the trails would be slippery, or in strong winds.*

Equipment: walking boots, warm clothing, long trousers, swimwear, sunhat, snacks, water

Transport: 🚌 103 or 138 (Arco bus). Ask for '**Vail**-yoh So-**lahr**' (the old *solar*); the stop is 1.7km northwest of Santana's town hall (150m north of Bragados Restaurant), 400m south of the Quinta do Furão road. Or 🚌 56 to Santana. Return on 🚌 103 from the Vigia turn-off at São Jorge; *be there at least 10min before departure time* from São Jorge. By 🚗: park in São Jorge or at the Vigia and take 🚌 103 or 138 *east* to the start.

Shorter walk: Santana — São Jorge. 7.5km/4.7mi; 2h37min. End the walk at São Jorge's church.

Refreshments en route:
Bragados restaurant (near the start)
Quinta do Furão (see pages 90-91)
bar/café at Calhau bathing area
bar in São Jorge

Points of interest:
Santana village
São Jorge's baroque church
old port of Calhau/bathing area

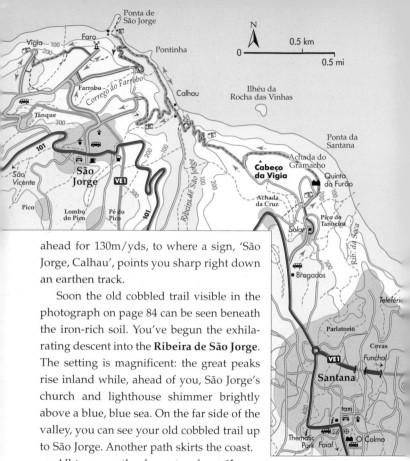

ahead for 130m/yds, to where a sign, 'São Jorge, Calhau', points you sharp right down an earthen track.

Soon the old cobbled trail visible in the photograph on page 84 can be seen beneath the iron-rich soil. You've begun the exhilarating descent into the **Ribeira de São Jorge**. The setting is magnificent: the great peaks rise inland while, ahead of you, São Jorge's church and lighthouse shimmer brightly above a blue, blue sea. On the far side of the valley, you can see your old cobbled trail up to São Jorge. Another path skirts the coast.

All too soon the descent ends; at **1h** you skirt to the left of a cheerful bar/restaurant and swimming pools with sun loungers, then cross an old bridge over the river. Turn right and follow the coastal path, past a well-kept house on the left, then one on the right. The rest of **Calhau** is in ruins, but it was once such an important port that it boasted both a church *and* a chapel! Part of an old wall, with remnants of tiles, still rises near the sea. Opposite the first of the ruins is a **tap** and the trail we'll climb later to São Jorge. The wide sea-side path takes you deliciously close to the pounding breakers. You pass a trail up to the left* and two minutes later come to a

View down to Calhau on the descent

deep and precipitous inlet just below the lighthouse (**1h20min**); ahead is a fishermen's bridge over to the **Ponta de São Jorge**. This area is often damaged by rock falls; leave it to the fishermen, and enjoy the view *from a distance!*

Return to Calhau (**1h40min**), then go up the steep trail by the tap. As you climb, look across to your descending trail, etched into the cliff on the far side of the river. By **2h15min** you will have huffed and puffed up to a junction. Cross half-left over the road and climb cobbled steps towards the cream-coloured walls of São Jorge's cemetery. Facing the **cemetery gate** (**2h25min**), turn right up a road, after seven minutes passing to the right of the chapel

*If you are pressed for time, you could use the map to shorten the walk, taking this path to go more directly to the Vigia (missing out São Jorge).

shown here. Continue round left to visit the magnificent church in the centre of **São Jorge** (**2h37min**; nearby bar/bus stop).

Walk back to the palm-shaded chapel and turn left. Ignore a road off right; continue ahead along the **Estrada Municipal do Farrobo.** Beyond a stream (**Corrego do Farrobo**), climb to a T-junction and turn right to the **lighthouse** (**3h**). Walk back from the lighthouse about 80m/yds, then turn right on a concrete walkway (red lettering 'Vigia'; arrow). When the concrete ends, follow a red earthen track past a track and then steps on the left. At a Y-fork go right; the track becomes a path and curls left, with vines to the right. You are aiming for the circular white building up ahead. At a T-junction, turn right to a road. Turn right again, to the **Vigia** ('look-out', once used by whalers; **3h25min**). From here the views west capture the attention, especially over Ponta Delgada's seaside church on a flat spit of land and the huge hotel, with Cabanas above and Ribeira da Janela in the distance. Take the road out to the Estrada Municipal do Farrobo (**3h30min**), to flag down a bus at the 'Vigia' signpost. *(To be on the safe side, arrive 10 minutes early!)*

The little chapel at São Jorge and the interior of the baroque church; left: maize drying on an old Santana house

Quinta do Furão

No doubt the best time of year to visit this five-star hotel is during the grape harvest in the autumn (when guests are encouraged to join in the grape pressing and ensuing festivities), but it's gorgeous all year round. If it's a fine day, no doubt you'll want to lunch outdoors on the lovely terrace. And you needn't expect to pay five-star prices if you just visit for a light lunch as described overleaf (or snack at the pub which opens an hour later).

Old wine press (above) and vineyards at the Quinta do Furão

Moreover, the menu boasts

restaurants

eat

QUINTA DO FURÃO
Achada do Gramacho, Santana
(291 570 100/101/102
www.quintadofurao.com
restaurant open daily, 12.00-15.30
and 19.00-21.30 €-€€€; pub 13.00-
22.00 €

huge menu, as befits a 5-star hotel

Specialities include

entrées: fish soup with celery and saffron, tomato and onion soup, limpets (see over), tomato and fresh Santana cheese in balsamic vinegar

fish: *espada* fillets with almonds or with banana and 'madeira' sauce (the latter being a combination of white wine, *sercial*, butter and garlic)

meat: *bife à Caldeirão Verde* (fillet steak done like beef Wellington, but with Roquefort cheese), *espetada*

While you wait: pickled tripe, pigs' ears and tuna ...

many regional specialities. We were pleasantly astounded, on our first visit, to be presented with the tray of nibblers shown above — titbits more likely to appeal to a Madeiran palate than an international clientèle! (These free hors d'oeuvres vary daily.) Naturally there is a very extensive wine list (the hotel is owned by the Madeira Wine Company); the Porta da Ravessa (an Alentejo) was dry and fragrant — a perfect accompaniment to our lunch of soup and grilled limpets.

One of Santana's oldest restaurants is at the hotel **O Colmo**, where in the past we have dined on memorable crayfish stews. Nowadays Colmo is usually packed with tourist coaches. Coaches also call at the Furão three days a week (days vary), so arrive at noon sharp!

Another good place for lunch is the lido bar/restaurant at **Calhau**, where you'll have this pretty view — perhaps after enjoying a swim.

LIGHT LUNCH AT QUINTA DO FURÃO

Tomato soup and country or 'house' bread (pão da casa)

The tomato soup recipe is on page 82 but note, in the photograph below, that the Furão leaves the onions in fine slices, *not* puréed.

For the bread, knead the starter dough, then knead in the potato purée and finally the flour. Add warm water as necessary to achieve an elastic consistency.

Cover and leave to rise overnight. Mould into an oblong loaf and cook in a hot oven (230°C, 450°F, gas mark 8) for 30 minutes (or until it sounds hollow when tapped).

Grilled limpets (lapas grelhadas)

Arrange the limpets on clean shells in a cast iron pan (as above) or any suitable grilling tray. Pour over the butter, lemon and garlic juice, and grill for just three minutes. Serve with 'country bread'.

Ingredients (for 4 people)

for the country bread
1 kg plain flour
200 g sweet potatoes, puréed
100 g starter dough (5 g yeast, 100 g flour, warm water, salt)

for the limpets
4 dozen limpets and clean limpet shells
150 melted butter
juice of one lemon
4 lemons (for serving)
garlic juice to taste

MEMORIES OF COLMO

We've no idea how the memorable crayfish stew was done at O Colmo many years ago, or whether they still make it. But this is a very easy recipe to make with limited cooking facilities when you are on Madeira — or to enjoy back home — *if* you can buy *really fresh* crayfish or lobster.

Crayfish stew
(caldeirada de langostins)

Melt the butter in a flameproof casserole or heavy-bottomed frying pan and then add the chopped onion and sliced carrot. Cover and simmer over a low heat for 10 minutes.

Stir in the mustard and add the crayfish (or shrimp). Pour over the cream and port or madeira; recover. Simmer gently over a low heat for about 15 minutes, until the shellfish is cooked.

Serve with boiled rice or boiled potatoes, 'country bread' and a green salad. Fabulous!

Ingredients (for 4 people)

1.5 kg uncooked crayfish, in the shells, but cleaned and slit open
110 g unsalted butter
1 small onion, finely chopped
1/2 carrot, finely sliced
1 tbsp Dijon mustard
200 ml double cream
200 ml red port wine or madeira wine

recipes

eat

Like Walks 3, 5, 8 and 13, this route follows a restored old zigzag trail — in this case one that clings precariously to a sugar-loaf cliff. From a distance the route looks impossible — and indeed it was for most people before the railings were built. Today the easy route lets you relax and savour the tremendous coastal views.

caminho da entrosa

WALK

9

The walk begins at the **church** in **Boaventura**: head southeast along the ER101 towards Santana. Continue along the road for 300m/yds, then turn left in front of the electricity substation, passing the **Solar de Boaventura** (see page 97) on your left.

Some 1.2km down this road, descend the path on the right, the '**Caminho do Calhau**' (**20min**). After crossing the **Ribeira do Porco** on a stone bridge, it's worth exploring the picturesque old **ruins** to the left, above the mouth of the river. You can either take the narrow path on the left through a red clay gully (an awkward scramble at the outset; the path is shown over-leaf) or bear right on the main path and, at a fork by another stone ruin, turn left. *We* think the ruins are the remains of an

Distance: 6.5km/4mi; 2h50min

Grade: moderate ups and downs of 370m/1220ft overall. You must be sure-footed, but there is no danger or danger of vertigo *provided that the sturdy railings are in place*.

Equipment: stout shoes or walking boots, warm clothing, sunhat, water, walking stick; swimwear in summer

Transport: 🚌 6 or 🚗 to/from Boaventura. Motorists can shorten the walk by 3km/45min: park at the Caminho do Calhau or the São Cristovão restaurant (we have not recommended this restaurant as we had very disappointing meals there). Or do as a one-way walk, ending at Arco and returning on 🚌 103 (quite easy, with an ascent of just 180m).

Refreshments en route:
Solar de Boaventura near the start of the walk (see page 97)
Snack Bar/Restaurante Arco (the halfway point or end; see page 97)

Points of interest:
beautiful old trail
ruined mill
mini-museum at the Solar

old textile mill: our Madeiran history book refers to such ruins in this area, where 'fabric was made using the red clay obtained nearby'. But the locals seem convinced it was a sugar mill.

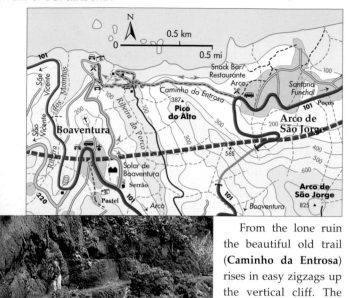

Red clay gully in the Ribeira do Porco

From the lone ruin the beautiful old trail (**Caminho da Entrosa**) rises in easy zigzags up the vertical cliff. The views straight down to the sea are breathtaking, but railings ensure no danger — unless they come down in storms (they *will* be repaired eventually; this is a popular walk with islanders proud of their heritage). Historians — who were probably carried round the sugar-loaf in hammocks — also marvelled at the huge houseleeks on these cliffs ('the size of hats').

The trail emerges at the **Snack Bar/Restaurante Arco** on the ER101 (**1h20min**; bus 6, 103, 132). After a break for refreshment, return the same way to **Boaventura** (**2h50min**).

Solar de Boaventura

Once a private manor house, then a school, then the health centre, this *solar* opened as an hotel in 1992 and expanded in 1998. Lovely public rooms with comfy sofas ranged round a mini-museum of artifacts — from an old loom and still to old telephones; cozy bar; gardens; two dining rooms — in the old house, with open fire, or the newer conservatory.

SOLAR DE BOAVENTURA
Boaventura (291 860 888
daily lunch and dinner €–€€€

ten **entrées**, including 'Entrada Solar' (swordfish, salmon, plain and smoked ham, egg, mixed shellfish, sardines, mayonnaise, cucumber, tomato and lettuce!)

soups and **omelettes**; **spaghetti**

fish *espada* (see page 99), sole, tuna, mixed grill, shellfish with rice or spaghetti

meats include steak, lamb chops, some imaginative pork dishes (including pork with fruit and curry), chicken

good selection of **cakes** and **tarts** — with or without **home-made ice cream**

SNACK BAR/RESTAURANTE ARCO
Arco de São Jorge, ER101 (no (available)
daily, all day €

soups and **sandwiches**

fish *espada*, octopus, parrot fish *(bobião)*

meats include steak, lamb or pork chops, beef stew with vegetables *(jardineira)*, chicken

---

Solar da Boaventura and the loom in the museum; below: Snack Bar/Restaurante Arco

restaurants

eat

SOLAR SPECIALITIES

Pork escalopes (escalopes de porco)

Season the pork escalopes with the crushed garlic, salt and pepper. Dust lightly with flour and gently fry in oil on a low heat, turning once, until golden.

Remove the escalopes from the pan, transfer to a warm plate and keep warm in the oven. Now use the same pan to make the sauce. Add the white wine and lemon juice and simmer this mixture until it reduces to make a syrupy sauce.

Pour the sauce over the meat and serve with boiled potatoes and vegetables — in the case of the Solar, three or four different vegetables in season!

Ingredients (for 4 people)
8 pork escalopes (about 800 g)
200 ml white wine
garlic, crushed, to taste
flour for dusting
oil of choice for frying
juice of 2 lemons
salt and pepper

recipes

eat

Espada pigalli (not shown)

Bring enough water to cover the fillets to a gentle boil; add the salt, pepper, garlic and parsley. Poach over a gentle heat for about 6-7 minutes. Keep warm.

For the sauce, use 200 ml of the cooking water and add the white wine, Pernod and cream. Simmer till it reduces to a smooth sauce.

'Filled' espada (*espada recheada*)

Immerse the fillets in the wine for 15min, then remove; set aside the wine. Season the fish with garlic, salt and pepper. Then dust with flour and fry in 1 tbsp oil for 6-7 minutes. Keep warm.

Make a sauce by gently warming the cream, mayonnaise and remaining wine; let thicken, add the prawns and simmer for a further couple of minutes. Pour over the fish.

Ingredients for both recipes (for 4 people)

8 fillets of *espada* (about 650 g)
200 ml white wine
garlic, crushed, to taste
salt and pepper

Ingredients for the individual recipes (for 4 people)

for the pigalli:
4 shot glasses of Pernod
2 tbsp fresh chopped parsley
100 g double cream

for the filled espada
200 g pre-cooked prawns
100 ml double cream
100 g mayonnaise

Power and majesty. These may be your first impressions of the Levada do Norte. You are at the centre of the north/south cleft that splits the island. The high peaks rise in the east; the magnificent valley of Serra de Água lies to the south. At your feet, 1.5m deep and just as wide, the levada surges along in a massive channel.

folhadal

WALK

Start the walk opposite the **Bar/Restaurante Encumeada**, on the south side of Encumeada Pass, where a sign indicates 'Folhadal'. Climb the concrete steps up to the **Levada do Norte** and follow it westwards, past the keepers' flower-filled house. You'll be amazed by the abundance of vegetation: conifers of every description, heath and hawthorn, with a tangle of laurel, azaleas, lilies, hydrangeas, and myriad wild flowers. If you're walking here in June, you'll see the splendid cornflower-blue 'Pride of Madeira' in all its glory.

In **12min** you come to the promontory of **Lapa do Galho**: from here you enjoy fine views down over the valley and the south coast. You can also see the levada continuing to the east and emptying into the metal pipe down to the Serra de Água

Distance: 8.5km/5.3mi; 2h50min

Grade: easy, but you must be sure-footed and have a head for heights (**danger of vertigo** on the Levada das Rabaças). Two tunnels (one fairly long). The Levada do Norte route is part of PR17 and may be waymarked.

Equipment: stout shoes, **good torch for each member of the party**, warm clothing, sunhat, water

Transport: 🚐 6 to/from Encumeada Pass (not the Residencial Encumeada). By 🚗: park at the viewpoint on the north side of the pass.

Short walk: Encumeada — Folhadal — Encumeada. 4km/2.5mi; 1h. Equipment, access/ return as above. Follow the main walk to Folhadal and back. **A 5-star walk on a fine day**; the paths are amply wide, and there is little danger of vertigo, but *good torches are essential.*

Refreshments en route:
Bar/Restaurante Encumeada (at the start)
Residencial Encumeada (1km south)
Pousada dos Vinháticos (3.5km south); *highly recommended*

Points of interest:
Levada do Norte and its tunnels
laurisilva
folhados (lily-of-the-valley trees)

power station (inaugurated in 1953). There are 50km/ 31mi of channels north of here (including 11km/6.8mi of tunnels). From the power station the water flows on in another 35km/22mi of channels (7km/4.5mi of tunnels) to irrigate the terraces of Ribeira Brava and Câmara de Lobos (see Walk 11, which follows a short stretch of the same levada before making for Cabo Girão).

Past the promontory, the levada forks (**14min**). Turn right and follow the Levada do Norte into the **tunnel**, which will take about 10-12 minutes to pass through. We'll never forget our first walk here: we approached the tunnel to find what looked like a washing machine gone mad. Thick white 'foam' was pouring out. It was fog, rushing through from the other side (as it often does: see the photograph on page 100)!

The tunnel exit (**25min**) frames your first glimpse of **Folhadal**, a 'museum' of ferns and indigenous trees — *vinháticos* (Madeiran mahogany), *til* trees (laurels) and white-barked *paus brancos* (olive family). But

Left: a *folhado*, the lily-of-the-valley tree native to Madeira. Above: on the levada to Folhadal

your eyes will be drawn to the *folhados* for which this wood is named — the summer-flowering lily-of-the-valley trees, native only to Madeira. Keep ahead through the ancient *laurisilva*, enjoying views to the São Vicente Valley — until you come to a **second tunnel** (**45min**).*

End the Folhadal route here and return the same way to the levada fork (**1h15min**). Now turn right to follow the narrower **Levada das Rabaças** (1970), a 'tributary' of the Levada do

*If you don't suffer from vertigo, have a *very good* torch — and plenty of time, you could follow the levada through this and two more tunnels, to a pretty waterhouse above the São Vicente Valley; allow 2h return (50min in tunnels). This is a wonderful, adventurous route through ancient woodlands; railings protect the most exposed sections.

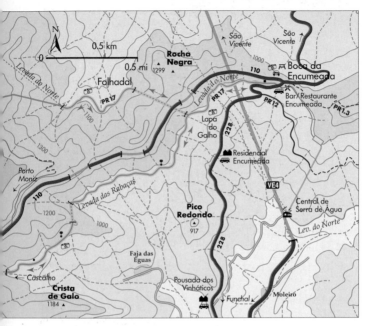

Norte. It is flowing in from Cascalho, an enormous basin pouring with waterfalls in the upper Ponta do Sol Valley — just one of the sources for this levada. In **1h45min** a **waterfall** on the right heralds a short **tunnel** (three minutes to pass). Seven minutes later, you reach a keepers' lonely house above the Pousada dos Vinháticos. In **2h** you come to a very long **tunnel** which eventually leads to Cascalho.

Turn back here, to the 'Folhadal' sign at **Encumeada** (**2h50min**), where the bus stops.

Vinháticos (top), Restaurante/Snack Bar Encumeada (left), Residencial Encumeada (right)

You have three good choices for lunch near the pass. The nearest is the **Snack Bar/Restaurante Encumeada** across the road. This is a simple, but very pleasant place, with a surprisingly ambitious menu.

Just 1km downhill is the beautifully sited **Residencial Encumeada**, with wide terraces, snack bar, and large dining room. A few guide books wax lyrical about the place and the hearty mountain fare. We've often stopped for a drink, but have been unlucky in our attempts to have a meal … or, indeed, even to get them to send a menu for this book!

Another 2.5km downhill is the **Pousada dos Vinháticos**. It's been one of our favourite places to stay for decades, our little piece of heaven (see over).

SNACK BAR/RESTAURANTE ENCUMEADA
(291 952 319
daily 08.30-22.00 €

entrées: vegetable or bread soup (*açorda*), giant prawns, grilled limpets

fish: *espada, bacalhau*

wide range of **omelettes**

meats: *parrilla Argentina* (a mixed grill), *espetada* on laurel skewers, *bife a Portuguesa* (steak with white wine, garlic and smoked ham), pork cutlet, *picado* (sautéed meat), *feijoada* (Brazilian bean stew; 24h notice required)

restaurants

eat

POUSADA DOS VINHATICOS

The *pousada* (the only one on the island) offers consistently imaginative and delicious regional, Portuguese and international dishes. *Do* spend a night here — in one of the three enchanting rooms in the old house or in the romantic 'log cabin' (give the annex a miss). Wake up to the sight of Crista do Galo, the beautiful 'cock's comb' ridge behind the building, and to the cheerful breakfast buffet.

The dining room, set for breakfast (top), and octopus salad

POUSADA DOS VINHATICOS
ER228 above Serra de Água (291 952 344; daily 12.30-21.30 €€-€€€

Frequently changing menu

a dozen **entrées**, ranging from smoked ham with seasonal fruit, octopus salad (see left), fried banana with bacon and five kinds of home-made soup

fish dishes are confined to *espada*, *bacalhau* and tuna, but with a variety of sauces; also a superb seafood gratin

meat dishes are outstanding for those tired of the usual fare. Of course there is *espetada*, but also roast pork loin with chestnuts, braised tongue, rabbit in wine, beef *pousada*-style (with mushrooms), delightful chicken with curry and coconut

very wide selection of **sweets** and excellent **wine list**

Braised ox tongue
(lingua de vaca estufada)

This is *not* the *pousada's* recipe (which is pictured right). It's just a dish we've been making over the years, using madeira wine. By the way, the sliced green vegetable is *pimpinela*, available in the supermarkets. Cook it like squash.

Cover the tongue with cold water. Add the bay leaf and onion. Bring to the boil, skim off any scum that rises to the top, then turn down the heat and cook gently until it reaches the consistency you like — perhaps 3 hours for slightly chewy, 4 hours for melt in the mouth. Drain and keep warm.

For the sauce, take 100 ml of the cooking water, add the wine and madeira wine, crushed garlic, cream and seasoning. Simmer, stirring, to reduce, until you have a shiny glazed sauce. Remove the skin from the tongue, slice it, and pour the sauce over. At its best with *garlic mash!*

Ingredients (for 4 people)
1.5 kg ox tongue
200 ml white wine
100 ml madeira wine
100 ml double cream
100 ml water from the cooked
   meat
2 cloves of garlic, crushed
1 bay leaf
small onion, peeled and stuck
   with 2 cloves
salt and pepper to taste

recipes

eat

This walk begins in a valley full of cherry trees before progressing above the island's most important terraced vineyards and moving on to the world-famous sea-cliff, Cabo Girão. If you're intrigued (not terrified) by the photograph above, you can swoop down to the coast in a cable car just west of Câmara de Lobos.

cabo girão

WALK

When the 96 bus roars up the hill at **Estreito**, you'll first pass the church and then a chapel on the left. Just round the next bend is the bus stop, called 'Levada (do Norte)'. **The walk starts** here: continue left uphill towards 'Jardim da Serra', ignoring the road to Castelejo and Boca dos Namorados to the right. After just 20m/yds turn left on the signposted levada, below photogenic vine-bearing trellises. It's hidden under concrete here, but you'll soon hear it singing underfoot. When a road crosses the levada, follow it for about 100m/yds, then find the open levada on the right.

Just as the levada bends right into the narrow **Ribeira da Caixa** (**20min**), *take two separate paths down left, a few minutes apart, to avoid narrow ledges with overhanging rock.* Soon you're deep in the valley; in May it is smothered in cherry blossom; by early June cherries will be for sale by the roadsides. You cross a tributary and then the main river (**45min**) on levada 'bridges'.

Distance: 12km/7.5mi; 4h05min

Grade: moderate; a few narrow stretches on the levada demand a head for heights. Little ascent. Overall descents of about 650m/2130ft

Equipment: stout lace-up shoes or walking boots, sunhat, warm clothing in cool weather, water

Transport: 🚌 96 to the levada crossing, 0.7km north of the church at Estreito de Câmara de Lobos; ask for the 'Levada do Norte' bus stop. Return on any bus from the main road at Câmara de Lobos.

Short walk: end the walk at **Cabo Girão** and return on 🚌 154; 7.5km/4.7mi; 2h30min

Refreshments en route:
Bar (after 1h05min)
Snack bars at Cabo Girão (2h30min) and the cable car (3h15min)
Bars, restaurants at Câmara de Lobos (end of the walk)

Points of interest:
Levada do Norte
terraced vineyards
Cabo Girão
Fajã das Bebras cable car
Câmara de Lobos village

Levada do Norte and typical chimney peeping through vine trellises

On leaving the valley, the church at **Garachico** comes into view below (**1h05min**). Five minutes later, take the *third* set of steps up to a road, where the levada is almost opposite (or take the *second* set of steps, to the signposted 'Bar' just uphill to the right, after which the levada is 25m/yds downhill). At **Nogueira**, the levada seems to end at a house (**1h35min**). Descend the concrete ramp/steps on the left and, when you meet a cobbled road, climb it to regain the channel. In six-seven minutes you cross the ER229 (**1h45min**) and take steps back down to the levada.

At **Cruz da Caldeira** (**1h55min**), the levada curls right, through a tunnel under Cabo Girão. *Keep ahead here,* alongside a narrow levada. Pass steps down left towards Câmara de Lobos and, 10 minutes later, turn right up *crossing steps,* to a road. Follow this through a huge, garish tourist complex to the breathtaking

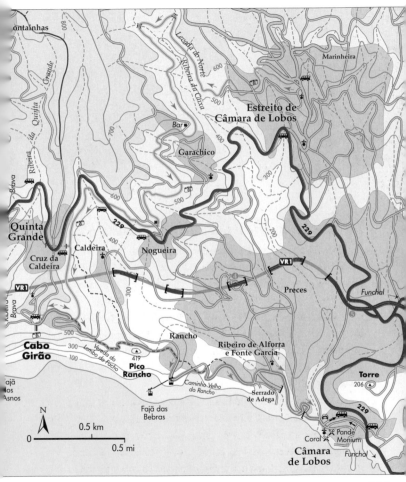

Cabo Girão and path from the cliff down towards Câmara de Lobos

Cabo Girão viewpoint (**2h30min**).

Then return to the steps you came up (by a small parking bay) and follow them downhill. This trail, with street lights, is called **Vereda do Lombo do Facho**. Meeting the road lower down, go left. Where the road curves left, descend concrete steps to the right (**2h50min**). In five minutes meet a narrow lane and follow it to the right. It quickly reverts to steps, and you pass a sign on a wall, '**Caminho Velho do Rancho**'. Five minutes down, meet another road: follow this to the right, to the end of the promontory at **Rancho**, where a **cable car** (**3h15min**) runs down to **Fajã das Bebras**, a landslip just east of the one below Cabo Girão.

Some 200m/yds downhill from the cable car turn right down short-cut steps. Rejoining the road (still Caminho Velho do Rancho), follow it to the right. Keep left at a Y-fork, then ignore a wide road to the right (a short-cut, but it goes through a tunnel). Soon you're in **Câmara de Lobos** (**4h05min**).

Madeira wines

Local wines from the *tinta negra mole* grape are fortified with grape brandy, heated in an *estufa* at 40-45 °C for three months, then matured in oak in warm cellars for at least five years. Four types are produced:

• *Sercial:* a pale dry *(seco)* aperitif wine, served slightly chilled

• *Verdelho:* a tawny, medium dry *(meio seco)* wine, at its best with soup, cheese, cake or fruit

• *Bual:* a nutty, medium-sweet *(meio doce)* dessert or cheese wine

• *Malmsey (malvasia):* a sweet *(doce)* after-dinner drink

When buying wine, ensure that the bottle bears the stamp of origin and quality issued by the Wine Institute of Madeira. We've often asked for a pre-prandial *sercial* — only to be offered a 'dry madeira' bearing no resemblance to the real thing!

Genuine madeiras can be sampled at the Madeira Wine Company (Av Arriaga 22), the Adegas de São Francisco (Av Arriaga 28 — next to the Tourist Office) for Blandy wines, and the Diogos Wine Shop (Av Arriaga 48) for Barbeito products.

Estreito: vine trellises over the Levada do Norte

113

Coral

Coral was first opened many years ago by a friend of ours who had trained at Reid's Hotel (and played for Marítimo!). At that time it was one of very few restaurants on the island with any 'style'. It was razed to the ground in 2004, to rise again on the new esplanade (with underground parking). It's very stylish, with stunning views to Cabo Girão. But the menu and cuisine lack the flair one might expect in such an up-market setting.

CORAL
on the esplanade (**291 942 469**
daily **10.00-24.00** €€

wide menu, from **soups, salads, omelettes** and **spaghetti** for a light meal

grilled fish is the speciality, also fish stew (*caldeirada*) and shellfish with rice (*arroz de mariscos*) for two; lobster thermidor; squid (*lulas*) on a skewer

meats — steaks, pork, chicken, *espetada*

good selection of **cakes/tarts**; Irish coffee

It took the new owner so many years to reopen after the town centre was rebuilt that we had to find another place. So we made for the front of the church and the strangely-named restaurant **Pande Monium** (€; Largo de São Sebastião, 3; (291 942 110; open daily from 10.00-22.00). It's super! There is a wide choice of omelettes, soups, great *pregos,* daily specials, roasts, outdoor tables (if you don't mind the noise), and it's very cheap. There is also a very pleasant, clean café on the esplanade opposite Coral, but with nothing to suit special dietary requirements.

restaurants

eat

Tuna with onions
(atum cebolado)

Marinate the tuna in the other ingredients for 3-4 hours. Fry the fish (turning once) and onions together in oil until golden. Set aside and keep warm.

Reduce the marinade (minus the bay leaf) in the pan, then return the fish and onions to the sauce and simmer for a minute or two.

Fried cornmeal (milho frito)

Sift the flour, then dissolve it in a bit of cold water. Bring all the other ingredients to the boil in 1.5 l water, then add the flour, stirring constantly until smooth.

Spoon the mixture into a *chilled* shallow dish and refrigerate, preferably overnight. Cut into cubes and fry in oil until golden. Drain on paper towels.

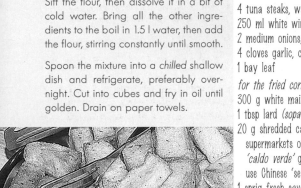

Ingredients (for 4 people)

for both recipes
salt to taste, oil for frying

for the fish
4 tuna steaks, washed
250 ml white wine
2 medium onions, sliced
4 cloves garlic, crushed
1 bay leaf

for the fried cornmeal
300 g white maize flour, sifted
1 tbsp lard *(sopa de banha)*
20 g shredded cabbage (sold in
    supermarkets on Madeira as
    'caldo verde' greens; at home
    use Chinese 'seaweed')
1 sprig fresh savoury

recipes

eat

This lovely ramble follows a narrow country road from Ponta do Pargo to Cabo and takes in a short stretch of the Levada Calheta–Ponta do Pargo. It's a favourite of ours — not only for the sea views, but because of the wonderful tea house/restaurant on the cliffs at Ponta do Pargo.

around ponta do pargo
WALK

Start the walk at the **church** in **Ponta do Pargo**. With the church on your left, walk left down the road signposted to Salão de Baixo, but turn right immediately, passing the **Casa do Povo**. *(Or, if you arrive at lunch time, first make for O Fio: keep straight down the Salão road to the cliffs. After lunch, return the same way but, just before the church, turn left.)* Ignore all paths off left. When you come to a crossing road (to the lighthouse), walk a few paces to the right uphill but, just before reaching the main ER101, go left downhill, passing a garage on the left with a tiled door frame. The road descends, crosses the **Ribeira dos Moinhos**, and rises into **Pedregal**, where you pass a **tap** on the right ('CMC'; **30min**).

Continue along the gently undulating road through flower-filled **Serrado** (notice the beautifully carved façade of a house on the right) and then

Distance: 10.5km/6.5mi; 4h

Grade: easy, with ascents/descents of 250m/820ft overall.

Equipment: stout shoes, sunhat, warm clothing in cool weather, snacks, water

Transport: 🚌 80 or 142 (or 🚗) to Ponta do Pargo. Return on 🚌 80.

Refreshments: O Fio at the cliff-top viewpoint 1km below Ponta do Pargo (15min down, 20min back up)

Points of interest:
lighthouse at the most westerly point on the island
O Fio! (See page 121.)

Special notes
The levada may be dry outside summer.
At press date a golf course (with hotel) was being built in this area; *the start of the walk may change in future* — as may the coastal landscape!
It is impossible to do the whole walk *and* enjoy a meal at O Fio if you are travelling by public transport. We would suggest first walking down to the restaurant, enjoying lunch, then heading back to the church to start the walk. End the walk on the EN 101 above Cabo, where bus 80 for Funchal passes at about 16.30. If you have time you can still explore a short way along the levada from there.

Levada Calheta–Ponta do Pargo

Lombada Velha, where a Canary palm graces the first house and a beautiful old manor stands off to the left, shaded by a huge eucalyptus. Beyond this hamlet keep left along an earthen track. It's worth forking left to the trig point at **Pico Vermelho**, for the view back to the lighthouse and Pico das Favas (with the antenna).

The track rises to a viewpoint and the chapel of **Nossa Senhora da Boa Morte** (**1h35min**). The chapel is unremarkable, but the grassy setting is idyllic — as the contented cows will agree! From the chapel follow the road uphill through **Cabo** to the ER101. Just *before* the main road, turn right on the **Levada Calheta–Ponta do Pargo** (a large water tank is on your left; **2h**). The levada crosses the main road in seven minutes (bus 80), then runs inland. Follow its meanderings

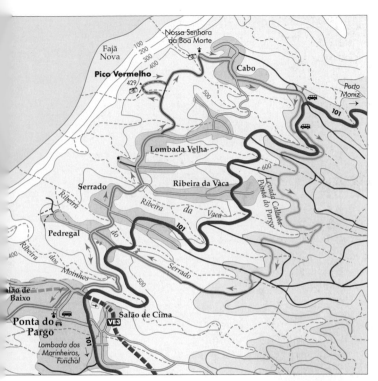

for under an hour. Four minutes after crossing the **Ribeira do Serrado** on a narrow levada 'bridge', turn right (**3h**) down a track (then road). Descend past a stone-crushing works to the ER101 (by a **tap** on the right), cross the road and continue straight down, back to the old road in **Pedregal**. Turn left; after 40m/yds you pass the **tap** encountered earlier. Retrace your steps to **Ponta do Pargo** (**4h**).

View north from the lighthouse of Ponta do Pargo

O Fio

On a rainy day there's nothing we like better than hopping on the morning bus and taking it all the way to Ponta do Pargo... just to enjoy our favourite meal. Then we can drink all the wine we like with lunch and nap on the bus back. But we've become so addicted to their *espada de vinho e alhos* that we even visit now on sunny days; no trip to Madeira is complete without this beautifully presented dish.

The photograph, taken from their garden, looks across to the viewpoint from where the old *fio* (goods hoist) lowered fruit and vegetables to ships bound for Funchal.

All the vegetables are really *fresh!* And the herbs for their special infusion are grown on pots around the terrace. In a nutshell: wonderful atmosphere whether you eat inside or out on the terrace, superb home cooking.

CASA DE CHÁ O FIO
Ponta do Pargo (**291 882 525**
daily ex Mondays 10.30-21.00 €€;
credit cards are not accepted!

many different **omelettes** or **soups** for a light meal; **sandwiches**, including vegetarian

various **petiscos** (savoury snacks) for two, or as an entrée: beef stew, chicken gizzards with curry, shrimps with garlic and parsley, octopus

fish *bacalhau*, octopus, shrimps, and their speciality — *espada de vinho e alhos* (see over)

meat dishes include pork stew with mushrooms, beef sauté *(picado)*, chicken giblets and gizzards *(moelas de galinha)*

specialities are teas (see over)

good **wine list**; we like the white Quinta do Cardo (Beira Interior)

restaurants

eat

121

O FIO SPECIALITIES

Espada with wine and garlic *(espada de vinho e alhos)*

This recipe works well back home with any moist white *fleshy* fillets (allow 8 minutes cooking time per 2.5 cm thickness). At O Fio they use fresh tomatoes, but tinned will do.

Season the fillets with salt and pepper. Marinate with the wine, tomato, garlic, bay leaf, and oregano for an hour. Remove from the marinade, dry the fish, then dust with flour. Heat 1 cm of oil to smoking in a heavy-bottomed frying pan, then reduce the heat a little. Fry the fish, turning once (about 6-8min).

<u>Ingredients (for 4 people)</u>
8 fillets of *espada* (about 750 g)
200 ml red wine
1 tin (400 g) chopped tomatoes
3 cloves garlic (crushed)
2 tbsp fresh oregano, chopped (or 1 tsp dried oregano
1 bay leaf
salt and pepper
flour to dust, oil for frying

Remove the fish, pat off the excess oil with paper towels, and set aside in a warm oven. Add the marinade to the oil, bring to the boil and simmer to reduce. Pour over the fish.

Serve as shown here! — with boiled potatoes, sweet potatoes (jacket-baked, then skin removed and sliced), salad, *feijoada* beans, onion rings, grated carrot and beetroot, lettuce and tomato.

recipes

eat

Bacalhau on sale in Funchal's market

Dried cod country-style
(bacalhau à moda do campo)

Dare you try your hand at *bacalhau*? These are the ingredients used at O Fio.

Soak the *bacalhau* in cold water for 24 hours, changing the water several times, to remove all the salt. Then soak in the fish in milk for an hour. Place the fish in just enough fresh simmering water (*do not let it boil!*) for about 15min, until tender. Carefully remove the skin and bones and flake into large pieces. Preheat the oven to 180°C, 350°F, gas mark 4.

Heat the olive oil in a heavy casserole, add the onions and cook until soft. Remove from heat; add the fish, potatoes, garlic and 1 tbsp of the coriander. Mix well.

Drizzle plenty of olive oil on top and bake, without a lid, until the top is golden — about 15min. To serve, sprinkle the rest of the fresh coriander on top.

Ingredients (for 4 people)

750 g *bacalhau* (dried salted cod; ask for centre cut or *lombo*)
500 g cooked sliced potatoes
2 medium onions, sliced
2 cloves garlic, crushed
250 ml olive oil
3 tbsp chopped fresh coriander

And for tea: marble, lemon or chocolate cake and their special infusion: lemon balm, peppermint, lemon, fennel, anise and sugar cane. Other sweets on the menu include home-made mango mousse or iced-cream cake (*semifrio de bolacha*)

There's no need to take a coach tour to see the island. You can 'do your own thing'; it is far less expensive, and the buses plying tourist routes are usually of coach standard. Here we suggest a way of seeing the western half of the island; you can see the eastern half with buses 56, 103 or 138.

'round the island'

EXCURSION

From Funchal bus 6 travels the 'old road' (ER229) via **Câmara de Lobos** and **Estreito** (Walk 11). Notice the huge Sousa building materials depot on both sides of the road in **Campanário**: it spreads its tentacles further each year — testament to the frenzied building on the island. Soon the road curls steeply down into **Ribeira Brava** — there is a fine overview on the approach. You may have time to take a quick peek at the lovely church, founded in the 1500s.

From here you travel north through a great cleft splitting the island east/west. After a fairly straight run along a narrow canyon graced with poplars, the old road (ER228) begins its winding ascent in earnest. Beyond **Serra de Água** you pass several incredibly beautiful viewpoints on the right, towards the **high peaks**, and then the **Pousada dos Vin-**

Description: an all-day trip, beginning in Funchal and travelling north from Ribeira Brava and over Encumeada Pass to São Vicente. From there along the north coast to Porto Moniz (5-hour break) and back via the south coast. **Important:** Rodo-este, the bus operator to the west, is promoting a circuit to Porto Moniz — out via the south coast and back through the Encumeada tunnel. *This is not recommended*, as it misses out the most spectacular pass on the island! Bus 6 leaves Ribeira Brava at 08.50; it might be worth taking a taxi there to start the tour at a more civilised hour!

Transport: Rodoeste 🚌 6 to São Vicente; leaves Funchal at 07.35(!); change to 🚌 150 (leaves at 10.25). Return from Porto Moniz on 🚌 80 at 16.00. *Tip: try to sit on the right-hand side of the bus for all journeys!*

Refreshments en route:
10min stop at Ribeira Brava
5h break at Porto Moniz
10min stop at Calheta

Points of interest:
valleys south and north of Encu-
    meada Pass
north coast, old north coast road
Porto Moniz and its lido
southwest coast, Calheta marina
splendid scenery throughout!

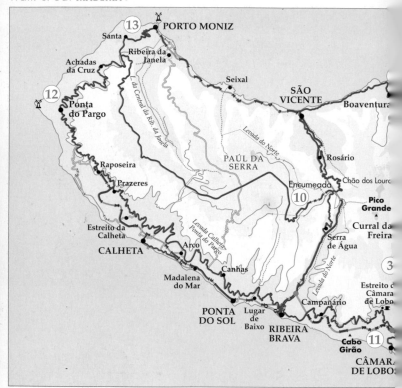

háticos (see pages 105-107), beautifully sited below a ridge — the aptly named **Crista de Galo** ('Cock's Comb'). Further uphill is the Residencial Encumeada, a very large hotel. The snaking ascent ends at **Encumeada Pass**, just at the centre of the island (1004m/3293ft). Look up to the left for views of the high plateau, the **Paúl da Serra**. Opposite the little restaurant here at the pass are

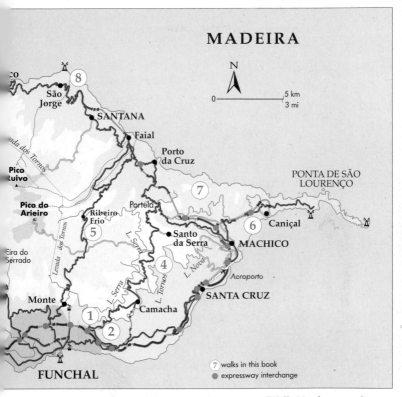

MADEIRA

N

0   5 km
     3 mi

steps up to the magnificent Levada do Norte (Walk 10; photograph page 100).

Then the bus descends into São Vicente's welcoming valley, past **Chão dos Louros**, a lovely laurel grove on the right, with fireplaces. Soon you'll have good views over **Rosário**'s church and stream: in high summer the hayricks weave ribbons of gold into the

Waterfall near São Vicente on the north coast road

tapestry of this emerald landscape. **São Vicente**, on the north coast, was one of the first villages on the island to be restored. In the 1980s the houses were repaired and painted in traditional Madeiran colours, the pathways recobbled, and landscaping was carried out. The bus gets here at about 09.40, so you have time to see the attractive old kernel of the village before bus 150 leaves at 10.25.

As Bus 150 leaves São Vicente, look out for the old chapel built into a hollowed-out rock south of the modern bridge, before heading west along the north coast and passing the waterfall shown left. Much of the route now runs through tunnels, but you will catch glimpses on the right of the 'Antiga ER101'— the old corniche road.

At **Seixal** the church perches high above the coast. Notice the steep vineyards here, edged with feathery heath-tree fencing to protect them from strong winds. Not far past Seixal, you should spot a palm-lined seaside promenade. Ahead lies **Ribeira da Janela**: the village takes its name from the 'window' *(janela)* in the 'sea-horse' rock just off the coast. Not far past a (perhaps still derelict) fish farm, you cross a bridge, pass a power station and go under a water pipe: this carries water from a very long levada in the bowels of the Paúl da Serra down to the power station.

At about 11.00 you're in **Porto Moniz**, where natural lava-rock pools have been beautifully incorporated into an extensive swimming complex with good facilities. You have time here for a five-hour break. But we'd suggest that you *stay on* the bus up to Santa, then return via Walk 13 and have lunch — perhaps at the **Restaurante Orca** or **O Cachalote**, by the pools (see page 133).

Heading out of Porto Moniz (either on the morning bus 150 or on bus 80 in the afternoon), the road climbs in steep hairpin bends, with magnificent views back over the village setting. Walk 13 begins 100m before the church in **Santa**. Further along, at **Achadas da Cruz**, there is a fantastic cable car (a 640m/2100ft descent), but unfortunately you can't see it from the main road.

The bus stops for 10 minutes at **Ponta do Pargo** but, alas, you won't be able to partake of the magnificent food at O Fio down on the cliffs (see page 121). The next stretch of road follow the contours in and out of shady valleys, sometimes crossing the lovely Levada Calheta–Ponta do Pargo, shown on page 118.

Beyond **Raposeira** and **Prazeres**, the route eventually heads towards the coast. At **Calheta** you descend past the church on the right and then a power station. Coming onto the seafront promenade (10 minute stop), there is a viewpoint on the right and the restored remains of an old *aguardente* (sugar cane spirit) factory to the left. But Calheta's main attraction it is marina and lido, with bijou sandy beaches either end.

After another inland stretch, via **Canhas**, you come into **Ponta do Sol**, where the church dates from the 15th century church and attractive façades face the seaside promenade. The bus stops again for 10 minutes at **Ribeira Brava**; time to buy some fresh fruit and veg at the nearby fresh-air market. Now it's time for a snooze, as the bus retraces your outward route through seemingly endless valleys, before arriving back in **Funchal** at about 8pm.

While road-building has ruined many of Madeira's old trails, several relatively short stretches still remain and have even been restored. Walks 3, 5, 8 and 9 all include sections of old cobbled trails. This descent to Porto Moniz, short as it is, offers magnificent views all the way down and intimate close-ups of country life.

to porto moniz

WALK

Start out on the main road in **Santa**, 100m/yds northeast of the church: just before the walled-in **cemetery**, turn left down **Caminho da Irmã do Perpetuo Socorro**. Go straight over two crossroads and, when the tar ends,continue down a *very steep* concrete lane, already enjoying the superb views shown left — over terraced fields and down to Porto Moniz and its large sea-water pool complex. When the concrete lane ends (**20min**), take concrete steps off right: these quickly give way to the old zigzag trail — much easier on the knees. The trail eventually runs into a valley — a pleasant shady interlude, before descending near the ER101.

Distance: 3km/2mi; 1h15min

Grade: moderate; a steep descent of 450m/1475ft. You must be sure-footed, but there is no danger of vertigo. *Virtually no shade*

Equipment: stout shoes (walking boots preferable), sunhat, water, walking stick, bathing things

Transport: 🚐 80 to Santa (10am departure) or 🚗: park by the WC, 100m northeast of the church. Return on 🚐 80 (16.00) or 139 (16.30) from Porto Moniz to Funchal (only bus 80 goes via Santa, if you left a car there).

Note for early birds: you can get to this walk and have more time in Porto Moniz if you take Excursion 2 (Transport details on page 125).

Refreshments en route:
bar/café in Santa and another at a viewpoint partway down the trail all facilities in Porto Moniz

Points of interest:
views down to Porto Moniz
old trail
sea-water pools at Porto Moniz

Ignore a minor road off to the right, and when you pass near the restaurant/viewpoint on the right (on the second hairpin bend), keep left downhill on another road. But after the hairpin bend to the right, watch for your turn-off left on a narrower, steeper cobbled trail. Concrete steps take you down to a narrow

The old trail to Porto Moniz

levada not far above the **school** in **Porto Moniz**.

Follow the levada to the right, then descend by road and steps (with street lights) to the **lido/pool complex** (**1h15min**). The bus leaves from the roundabout just above the pools. The **Residencial Orca** is on the far side of the roundabout, but there is a very large choice of restaurants and café-bars in the village.

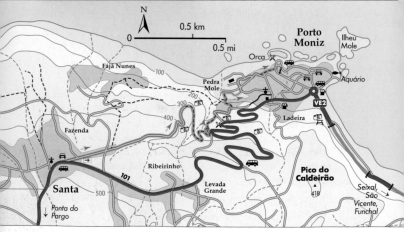

Restaurante Orca

Perched just above the sea-water pools and lido, for years the Orca was *the* place at Porto Moniz. It was certainly pleasant to spend the night here, as the sea-side rooms had huge terraces. Unfortunately the hotel is closed until they can afford to refurbish it, but the restaurant is as popular as ever — with good food and terrific views!

The Orca *does* cater for coach parties, but don't let this put you off. There is a veritable army of staff waiting to serve, and the coach guests (most of whom arrive just after 1pm) are seated in a different part of the dining room. Either go in for lunch at noon (ahead of the coaches) or after you've finished Walk 13 (when they should have gone).

> **RESTAURANTE ORCA**
> Porto Moniz (by the pools)
> (291 850 000
> **Daily 12.00-15.30; 19.00-21.30 €–€€**
>
> large menu, with light and more substantial meals
>
> **entrées** include 8 cold dishes, three soups, five omelettes
>
> excellent **fish**, the usual *espada*, but with different fruits, *cherne* (stone bass), tuna with *milho frito*, parrotfish, grouper, sea bream, trout, salmon, sole, *bacalhau*
>
> **meats** include beef, pork and lamb chops, roast chicken, beef with dates, *espetada* with *milho frito* and salad

Among the other restaurants at Porto Moniz is **O Cachalote** ((291 853 180), perched above the *natural* sea-water pools in a fabulous setting. It's only open for lunch and, like Orca, much visited by coach parties. The **Residencial Salgueiro**, opposite Orca on the far side of the roundabout (with a large souvenir shop below), is open daily for lunch and dinner ((291 850 080), but its setting can't compare with Orca's or Cachalote's.

restaurants

eat

FISH SOUP AT ORCA

Fish soup *(sopa de peixe)*

Cut or tear the fish fillets into mouthful-sized chunks as shown in this photograph taken at Orca. (Make sure no bones remain.)

In a large heavy-bottomed saucepan, fry the onion and garlic lightly in the oil. Add the stock and bring to the boil. Turn down the heat, stir in the tomato purée, then add the potatoes. Cook just below boiling for 6 minutes, then add the carrots and peppers and cook for another 6 minutes.

<u>Ingredients (for 4 people)</u>

300 g *espada* fillet (or other fairly solid fish)
2 potatoes, in large cubes
1 small onion, finely chopped
handful of finely-sliced carrots
2 tbsp finely-diced red peppers
1.5 l vegetable stock
two tbsp tomato purée
spices to taste: crushed garlic, bay leaf, clove, allspice, parsley
1 tbsp wine vinegar
20 ml olive oil

Remove half of the potatoes and whizz with a little stock; set aside. Add the fish, vinegar and spices to the soup and continue cooking for about 4 minutes (until the fish is cooked, but still in solid pieces). Then stir the puréed potatoes back into the soup to thicken.

This soup is especially good served with *pão da casa* (see page 92), which is often drizzled with olive oil rather than spread with butter.

recipes

eat

Transport: bus operators and web sites

Only journey times and some last return buses are shown. See web sites (**H**: www.horariosdofunchal.pt; **R**: www.rodoeste.pt; **S**: www.sam.pt) for full timetables and pages 12-13 for details of town bus passes. Departure points for all buses are shown on the plan inside the front cover.

Excursion 1: frequent town buses to return. **H**

Walk 1: frequent town buses for access and return. **H**

Walk 2: frequent town buses for access and return. **H**

Walk 3: journey time for bus 81 is about 45min. See the Horarios web site; only buses coded b), c) or e) call at the Eira do Serrado. **H**

Walk 4: journey time for bus 129 or 77 about 45min to Camacha, 1h from Santo da Serra (bus 77). Last 77 return bus 18.00 or 20.30+. **H**

Walk 5: best outgoing bus is 56; journey time about 50min; only suitable return is bus 103 at 18.35. **H**

Walk 6: bus 113 for access and return; journey time about 1h10min. **S**

Walk 7: bus 53 or 78 journey time 1h15min; last bus from Portela at 18.50+ (bus 53). **H**

Walk 8: bus 56 or 103 journey time to Santana 2h10min; last return from Arco de São Jorge bus 103 at 16.30. **H**

Walk 9: bus 6 journey time 3h10min to Boaventura; 4h to Arco. Returns up till 17.50 from Arco; 18.05 from Boaventura. **R** Also bus 103 from Arco at 16.30. **H**

Walk 10: bus 6 (07.35); journey time 2h; bus 6 at 16.00 to return. **R**

Walk 11: frequent 96 buses to go and many coastal return buses. **R**

Walk 12: bus 80 a much faster service (2h20min) than 142 (4h), but 142 arrives at noon and 80 at 12.20. Last return bus (80) at 16.35. **R**

Excursion 2: buses 6 and 80 run daily except Christmas Day; bus 150 runs daily except 25, 26, 31 Dec, 1 Jan and Good Friday. **R**

Walk 13: bus 80 (10.00)+; journey time 2h15min; bus 80 or 139 to return. **R**

+Mon-Fri only

TRANSPORT

We've been visiting Madeira for many years, doing what we like most — walking, eating and enjoying the Portuguese wines. Only in the last decade have excellent restaurants opened all over the island; in the past good food was limited to Funchal and just a few countryside establishments that still exist and are mentioned in this book.

About 15 years ago John was diagnosed coeliac and, more recently, lactose intolerant. Food intolerances are becoming ever more common, and we know *there are a lot of you out there!* Even if you have learned to cope at home, it can be very daunting to go on holiday. *Will the food in restaurants be safe? Will I be able to buy gluten- and dairy-free foods?*

If you suffer from food intolerance you have probably already learned at home that what initially seems a penance in fact becomes a challenge and eventually a joy. We eat far healthier meals now than we did before, with fewer additives. Nowhere is this more enjoyable than around the Mediterranean and on Madeira, where olive oil, fish, tomatoes and 'alternative' grains and flours are basic to the diet. Many, many dishes are *naturally* gluten- and dairy-free.

Of course food intolerances *are* restrictive — in the sense that we have to carry, buy or bake gluten-free breads and sweets, and we always need access to dairy-free 'milk', 'cream', 'yoghurt' and 'butter'. So over the years we've sussed out eating gf, df on the island, and it's *so simple*.

EAT GF, DF

EATING IN RESTAURANTS

The most common **first courses** are soup, fish and salads. Soups are *not* thickened with flour and very few contain cream — even though they look and taste 'creamy'. The secret is that they are thickened with a potato or vegetable (often pumpkin) purée.

The most popular **main courses** are grilled fish, steaks and chops. Sauces *(molhos)* usually consist of wine, tomatoes, onions, herbs and garlic, all reduced. If you are a sauce addict, like John, it is safer to *ask* (see inside back flap for help in Portuguese, although the staff usually speak English); you are likely to be pleasantly surprised. *Fried* fish is invariably dusted with flour (otherwise it is more difficult to cook), but just *ask*: they are happy to do it for you without flour — or take your own flour with you. All the restaurants recommended here cook meals individually; the staff are always accessible. For instance, our super-favourite fish meal, at O Fio, illustrated on page 122, was fried *without* flour (but still retained its shape).

We are always too full to have **dessert** but, if you have a sweet tooth, make for the restaurants on pages 42-43; the chestnut cake is 100% gf, df and out of this world. All restaurants offer fruit (including many exotic fruits) for dessert, and some have gf, df chocolate dishes (made with dark chocolate); *ask!*

SELF-CATERING

While many hotels on the island cater for food intolerances, we discovered the joy of self-catering years ago. What a liberation! Room to swing a cat (or, more likely, chop up a rabbit). Tables where you can spread out your maps and bus timetables. Sofas to loll about on with a good book on a rainy day.

But if we're staying in self-catering for a couple of weeks or more, we *do* treat ourselves to the odd night at one of the beautifully-sited hotels mentioned in this book. It's relatively easy to cope for just a night or two, even if they don't have the supplies. They will let you use their fridges (just take a carrier bag or container and label with your name and room number); the non-perishables can stay in your room.

Gf, df shopping

Madeiran supermarkets have no gluten-free products, except for the *naturally* gf flour used on the island, corn meal (*farinha de milho*). They do, however, usually have a huge stock of dairy-free goodies (usually Alpro, sometimes Provamel) — soya and rice milk, soya margarine, soya cream, soya sweets. (*Do not fall for* 'Planta', a spread available in all supermarkets which claims to be '*100% vegetal*', but in fact contains whey!)

There are two main **health food** shops in Funchal, both of which cater for food intolerances (and vegetarians).

Bio-Logos at 34 Rua Nova de S Pedro, (291 236 868 (40 on the plan, not far from Londres restaurant) is definitely the best. Rui, the helpful manager, speaks English (you can e-mail him in advance: bio.logos@mail.telepac.pt). On the ground floor there is a **vegetarian café-restaurant** called Ao Natural; downstairs there's a wide range of **gf bread** (including Schär), breakfast cereals, biscuits, cakes and pastas. Several brands are not yet known in England — a good opportunity to sample! Of course there are all kinds of long-life dairy-free milks and sweets, but check out the fridge: there are usually three different df **cheeses**, plus the French df spread called 'Rapunzel' — so good for spreading and frying (it doesn't burn).

Bioforma at 31 Rua Queimada de Cima, (291 229 262 (39 on the plan) is also well stocked, with most of the items listed under Bio-Logos (though they don't have cheese and often there's no df margarine). The selection is on the lower ground floor, where there is also a small **vegetarian deli**. In the freezer they keep a gf loaf made on the island (ask for it at the deli counter). But why not buy your bread direct from the bakery, a stone's throw away (see panel). Unfortunately, the staff at Bioforma are not at all helpful, and we have called twice (in different years) on 'stocktaking days', when we were not even allowed downstairs to buy anything — potentially a real worry.

FABRICA DE STO ANTONIO
Travessa do Forno 27-29 **(corner of 5 Outubro; 16 on the plan)** (291 220 255

This wonderful old bakery (founded in 1893) makes fresh gf bread on Thursdays and Fridays (but there is always some in stock). Their main customer for gf is the Savoy Hotel. You could phone and order in advance; when you collect it, buy some gf biscuits as well (a large selection in stock, but *not* dairy-free!). The bread keeps well out of the fridge and is very good toasted or *untoasted*. Contains rice and tapioca flour, corn and potato starch, egg whites, corn gum, oil, yeast, sugar, salt and vinegar.

Gf, df cooking

We've made all the **recipes** in this book using gluten- and dairy-free ingredients. Basically we just used a 1:1 substitution, and the cooking method was unchanged.

One of the recipes ('Reid's Cake', see pages 36-37) was in fact originally a gluten- and dairy-free recipe from Dietary Specials (www.nutritionpoint.co.uk). If you make it using normal wheat flour, we can only hope it tastes as good!

The only problem we have is *frying*, when the recipe calls for a mixture of oil and butter (or just butter). Most 100% vegetable spreads spit all over the place because they contain so much water. The best spreads (like the French Rapunzel) contain 60% sunflower oil, some palm and perhaps coconut oil; water *should rank no higher than third* on the list of ingredients. Note, too, that lard *(sopa de banha)* is widely available on the island.

CONVERSION TABLES

Weights		Volume		Oven temperatures		
						gas
10 g	1/2 oz	15 ml	1 tbsp	°C	°F	mark
25 g	1 oz	55 ml	2 fl oz			
50 g	2 oz	75 ml	3 fl oz	140°C	275°F	1
110 g	4 oz	150 ml	1/4 pt	150°C	300°F	2
200 g	7 oz	275 ml	1/2 pt	170°C	325°F	3
350 g	12 oz	570 ml	1 pt	180°C	350°F	4
450 g	1 lb	1 l	1-3/4 pt	190°C	375°F	5
700 g	1 lb 8 oz	1.5 l	2-1/2 pt	200°C	400°F	6
900 g	2 lb			220°C	425°F	7
1.35 g	3 lb			230°C	430°F	8
				240°C	475°F	9

MENU ITEMS

abacate avocado

abóbora marrow, pumpkin

açorda bread soup with garlic

água water

com gás sparkling

sem gas still

aguardente sugar cane spirit

alcaparras capers

alecrim rosemary

alface lettuce

alho garlic

amêijoas cockles

amêndoa almond

ananás pineapple

arroz rice

de mariscos rice with shellfish

assado(a) roast

atum tuna

aziete olive oil

azeitonas olives

bacalhau dried salted cod

batata potato

doce sweet potato

bife beef (or steak, as in bife de atum — tuna steak)

filete fillet

lombo sirloin

bodião parrotfish

bolo cake

do caco flat bread

do mel molasses cake

borrego lamb

bravo(a) wild

cabrito baby goat

calamares squid

caldeirada stew (usually fish)

camarão shrimp, prawns

caril curry

carne meat (usually pork)

caseiro(a) home-made

castanha chestnut

cebola onion

cerveja beer

chá tea

cherne stone bass

chouriço spicy pork sausage

coelho rabbit

cogumelos mush-rooms

corvina a local fish

costeleta cutlet

cozido(a) boiled (also: meat and vegetable stew)

do dia daily special

dose portion

dourada dory

enguia eel

ervas herbs

espada a local fish

espadarte swordfish

esparguete spaghetti

espetada beef cubes on a skewer

em pau de louro on a laurel stick

faisão pheasant

farinha (wheat) flour

fatia slice

favas broad beans

feijoada stew with (haricot) beans

fiambre cooked ham

fígado liver

frango chicken

frito(a) fried

funcho fennel

galinha hen

gambas giant prawns

garoupa grouper

gelado ice cream

grelhado(a) grilled

lagosta lobster

langostins crayfish

lapas limpets

legumes vegetables

leitão suckling pig

leite milk

lentilhas lentils

limão lemon

lingua tongue

linguado sole

lombo loin, sirloin

louro bay (laurel)

lulas squid

maça apple

maionese mayon-naise

manga mango

manteiga butter

de alho garlic butter

maracujá passion fruit

marisco shellfish

massa pasta (or pastry casing)

mel honey

melão melon

mexilhões mussels

milho cornmeal

frito fried

mista/mistura mixed

molho sauce

manjerona majoram

mostarda mustard

natas cream

nozes nuts

oregão oregano

ovo egg

pão bread

pargo sea bream

pastel small tart

pepino cucumber

peixe fish

picado, picadinho
sautéed meat
picante hot
peru turkey
pimenta pepper
(spice)
pimento pepper
(vegetable)
piri-piri hot red
pepper sauce
polvo octopus
porco pork
presunto smoked
ham
pudim crème
caramel
quiejo cheese
da serra fresh
mountain cheese
quente hot (as in
warm, not spicy)
recheado(a) stuffed
salmão salmon
salsa parsley
sande sandwich
sardinhas sardines
semilha potato
sidra cider
sopa soup
sumo juice
tarte tarte, pie
tomilho thyme
tosta toast(ed)
sandwich
toucinho bacon
trigo wheat
truta trout
vaca cow
vinho wine (see
pages 8, 113)
vitela veal

SHOPPING TERMS

apple *maçã*
avocado *abacate*
bacon *toucinho*
bay leaves *louro em
folhas*
beans *feijão*
beef* *bife*
beer *cerveja*
bread *pão*
broad beans *favas*
butter *manteiga*
cabbage *couve*
cake *bolo*
carrot *cenoura*
cheese *queijo*
cherries *cerejas*
chestnut *castanha*
chicken *frango*
cider *sidra*
cockles *amêijoas*
cod, dried *bacalhau*
coffee *café*
cornmeal *milho*
crayfish *langostins*
cream *natas*
cucumber *pepino*
dates *tâmaras*
eel *enguia*
eggs *ovos*
fennel *funcho*
fish *peixe* (many are
unfamiliar; see
'Menu items'
above)
flour *farinha*; maize
flour *milho*
fruit *fruta*
garlic *alho*
grapes *uvas*

ham, cooked
fiambre; smoked
presunto
herbs *ervas*
ice cream *gelado*
juice *sumo*
lamb* *borrego*
lard *sopa de banha*
lemon *limão*
lettuce *alface*
limpets *lapas*
liver *figado*
lobster *lagosta*
mango *manga*
marjoram *manje-
rona*
marrow, pumpkin
abóbora
melon *melão*
milk *leite*
mushrooms *cogu-
melos*
mussels *mexilhões*
mustard *mostarda*
nuts *nozes*
octopus *polvo*
olive oil *aziete*
olives *azeitonas*
onion *cebola*
orange *laranja*
parsley *salsa*
pear *pêra*
peas *ervilhas*
pepper *pimenta*
pig, suckling *leitão*
pineapple *ananás*
pork* *(carne de)
porco*
potatoes *batatas,
semilhas*; sweet
batatas doces

prawns *camarão*
giant *gambas*
passion fruit
maracujá
rabbit *coelho*
rice *arroz*
rosemary *alecrim*
salmon *salmão*
salt *sal*
sardines *sardinhas*
sausage, spicy
chouriço
sole *linguado*
soup *sopa*
spinach *espinafre*
spices, condiments
condimentos
squid *calamares*
sugar *açucar*
swordfish *espadarte*
tea *chá*
thyme *tomilho*
tomato *tomate*
tongue *lingua*
beef *de vaca*
trout *truta*
tuna *atum*
turkey *peru*
veal *vitela*
vegetables *legumes*
vinegar *vinagre*
wine *vinho*
water *água*
plain *sem gás*
sparkling *com gás*

*cuts of meat
cutlet, chop
costeleta
loin, sirloin *lombo*
filet *filete*

bold type: photograph; *italic type:* map

Third edition © 2012
Published by Sunflower Books
PO Box 36061, London SW7 3WS
www.sunflowerbooks.co.uk

ISBN 978-1-85691-387-4

Cover photograph: hummingbird on 'pride of Madeira' blossom

Photographs: John Underwood except for the cover: Dreamstime
Maps: Sunflower Books, adapted from Portuguese IGC and military maps
Series design: Jocelyn Lucas
Cookery editor: Marina Bayliss
A CIP catalogue record for this book is available from the British Library.
Printed and bound in China by WKT Company Ltd

Before you go ...
log on to
www.sunflowerbooks.co.uk
and click on '**updates**', to see if we have been notified of any changes to the routes or restaurants.

When you return ...
do let us know if any routes have changed because of road-building, storm damage or the like. Have any of our restaurants closed — or any new ones opened *on the route of the walk?* (Not Funchal restaurants, please; these books are not intended to be complete restaurant guides!)

Send your comments to mail@sunflowerbooks.co.uk